Managing Social Care
A Guide for New Managers

Paul Harrison

RHP

Russell House Publishing

Russell House Publishing
First published in 2006 by:
Russell House Publishing Ltd.
4 St. George's House
Uplyme Road
Lyme Regis
Dorset DT7 3LS
Tel: 01297-443948
Fax: 01297-442722
e-mail: help@russellhouse.co.uk

A catalogue record for this book is available from the British Library.

British Library Cataloguing-in-publication Data:

ISBN: 978-1-905541-00-3

Typeset by TW Typesetting, Plymouth, Devon
Printed by Biddles Ltd, King's Lynn

About Russell House Publishing

Russell House Publishing aims to publish innovative and valuable
materials to help managers, practitioners, trainers, educators and
students.
Our full catalogue covers: social policy, working with young
people, helping children and families, care of older people, social
care, combating social exclusion, revitalising communities and
working with offenders.
Full details can be found at www.russellhouse.co.uk and we are
pleased to send out information to you by post. Our contact
details are on this page. We are always keen to receive feedback
on publications and new ideas for future projects.

Contents

For my father, Michael Harrison
He would have been well impressed

About the Author

Paul Harrison has over thirty years experience of working in social care. He started out as a volunteer with the Simon Community. After qualifying as a social worker in 1978 he gained extensive experience in the areas of child protection and welfare services, alternative care, family support, homelessness, mental health and addiction. He has held a number of management positions within social care and is currently Director of Services for Children and Families in the Health Service Executive, North Dublin. He has also served on the board of management of a variety of voluntary organisations.

Paul holds an M.Litt. from Trinity College Dublin for research in social care and a Diploma in Healthcare Management from the Institute of Public Administration, Dublin.

Acknowledgements

I am fortunate to have had access to a number of great libraries while researching this book. Thanks to Fingal Libraries (Howth Branch), Dublin, which keeps a nice collection of management and associated material; to the National Library of Ireland which can turn up anything Irish; to Trinity College Dublin which generously offers excellent reading facilities to alumni undertaking research; to the Health Service Executive, Shared Service Library at Dr. Steevens' Hospital, Dublin, for a great collection of books, and on-line journals; to the Institute of Public Administration, Dublin, for a treasure trove of management material, and to Betty Cohen and all in the Social Work Library and O'Neill Library, Boston College, MA., for their hospitality and assistance.

Thanks also to Prof. Robbie Gilligan, Trinity College Dublin, for his encouragement and advice; to Maureen Browne, Michael Bruton and Mary Meyler for reading manuscripts and for their helpful suggestions; and to Mary Ahern, my wife, for her feedback and support.

Over my career I have worked to a myriad of managers. Some were inspirational; others were not. Yet there is learning in every reporting relationship and I would like to thank all of them because I learned something from each and every one.

Finally, thanks to Geoffrey Mann and all at Russell House Publishing for affording me the opportunity to publish this work.

Introduction

The first step into management

That first step into management is not easy. Most new management appointees in social care will not have any management training and they develop their skills on the job as they go along. Colleges are good at keeping up with examples of good practice, but they specialise in turning out good practitioners not good managers. Therefore this book aims to present newly appointed social care managers, or those with no formal management training, with practical advice to enable them to do the job more effectively.

The management task

Managing social services is not enormously different from other types of management. There are tasks that are common to both, such as the recruitment, motivation and supervision of staff, managing resources, planning and co-ordinating activities and monitoring results (Austin, 2002). Although management theory can be applied generally to any type of management this book focuses exclusively on the management of social care, and all the examples are taken from this source.

Mainstream management literature is aimed at marketing and the business of profit making. Marketing is about identifying opportunities and making money from them. Social care is, by and large, not for profit and usually the service is demand led so you are not out beating the bushes looking for business. However, that does not mean that ideas cannot be imported from the business world and used to good effect. Of course they can; for example it is commonplace nowadays to encounter concepts such as efficiency, effectiveness and value for money in the context of social care (Harlow and Lawler, 2002).

Managing social care

Yet social services do have some unique features. For one thing the business is never ending. It does not turn out a product; rather it is concerned with the ongoing process of meeting social need. Unlike goods, the service has no shelf life but is consumed on the spot (Austin, 2002). Social care is continuous in nature and an intervention with a particular individual, family or community could last for several years. Therefore some milestones need to be built in along the way to measure progress, and to know when to stop.

Another feature is that most social care staff are trained to be advocates for their clients. They have a dual loyalty to their employing organisation and their profession (Austin, 2002). They tend to talk of the service organisation in the third person, like people in a bar talk about the Government. This free sprit can also manifest itself in the decision making process. There is quite a prevalent culture of democracy where decision-making is often invested in the team rather than the manager. Like the idealism of youth, one does not want to crush it, but it may require a little guidance and direction. The first thing a new social care manager needs to learn is that *they* are in charge.

Moving from practitioner manager

The first big challenge upon appointment is to manage the transition from practitioner to manager. For example, a colleague was interviewing staff for a supervisory position. It was an internal competition so she knew all the candidates well. She tried to put one man at ease by throwing him a soft question at the start: 'Well John, what interests you in this particular position?' He looked bewildered and replied: 'Gosh, you have me there!' You would be surprised at how many people do not ask themselves the obvious question; why do I want this job? This is especially so when it comes to promotional opportunities and management positions. Most practitioners with a good track record of achievement reckon they deserve to be managers because they are good at what they do. However, when they attend for interview they are not being interviewed about their professional ability; they are being interviewed to establish whether they have the capacity to be a good manager.

Like so many other people I learned this lesson the hard way. I was a caseworker and applied for a job as a social work manager. My approach to the interview was to convince the interview board that I was a good caseworker and therefore deserved to be a manager. Fortunately, a kind old mentor took me aside and said: 'Paul, you've got to read the job description. That tells you what the job is all about'.

Therefore, this book sets out to help you make that first step from practitioner to manager. It tells you things I would like to have known when I started out, but had to discover for myself along the way. It explains how to get off to a good start as a manager, how to go about managing the service, how to manage people, the future, quality, change, and yourself. It does not promise to fix you or do it all for you; neither is it an academic tome. Rather, it is a fairly light read that leaves you free to take on board what you like and to disregard what you do not consider relevant. After all, social care is all about helping people to help themselves!

Chapter 1

Managing the First Few Weeks

Courage is being scared to death but saddling up anyway.

John Wayne

Step one; you *are* the boss now, so start getting used to it. This does not mean that you should adopt a Napoleonic stature and swan into the office in search of acclaim. No, do not, under any circumstances, undergo a personality change. Be yourself; that is why you got the job. It is more likely in the first few weeks that you will feel a little nervous and unsure. Undoubtedly your transition into management represents a major change. It will require learning new skills and dealing with unfamiliar challenges. However, console yourself in the knowledge that your professional skills do not become redundant now that you are a manager and that you will still be able to draw upon them.

Nearly half a century ago Greenwood (1957) identified five criteria that distinguish social work as a profession, and these have equally valid application to other areas of social care:

1. The extent to which the knowledge employed is based on a systemic body of theory.
2. The degree of development of, and commitment to, professional authority.
3. Attainment of community sanction for what is done.
4. An ethical code.
5. Values, norms and symbols of a professional community.

Neither your professional skills nor your value base will be affected by your role as manager. In fact those who you manage may well be looking out to see if you have retained them.

Bringing your professional skills into management

A key task for the social care manager is to reconcile organisational demands and professional values (Weinbach, 1994). So, be assured that you will not have to abandon your professional values as you take on a management role. However, it is a fact that the further up the career ladder a social care professional climbs, the more generic management skills replace professional skills until at last a professional, like Caesar, might be accused of scorning the base degrees from which they did ascend. Even if the social care community does disown you, you will retain some of your professional competencies that will stand to you as a manager. It has been said that, regardless of the setting, there are three components of knowledge in social care (Brown, 1996):

1. Knowledge that informs practitioners of client's experience and context.
2. Knowledge that helps the practitioner plan appropriate interventions.
3. Knowledge that clarifies the practitioner's understanding of legal, policy, procedural and organisational context.

You will bring this knowledge with you into your management role. Indeed many of your skills will travel with you and will provide you with a fundamental management toolkit. Chiefly among these is an ability to assess situations and make decisions, which is a critical component of good management. Your training will also assist you in assessing individuals, which is another critical management task. Your ability to listen empathetically will stand to you. Social care workers are good at allowing people space to tell their story.

You will also retain an advocacy role, taking a stand on important social issues and representing the interest of the client to staff, the organisation and the outside world. Advocacy will also apply when you make a case for more resources, such as money, co-operation, support and time. You will also draw on your communication skills to assess interactions, to collaborate and to problem solve.

As a manager you will, more than ever, have to make brave decisions by taking calculated risks that may not always work out. You will draw on your knowledge of task-centred work by managing for results and evaluating outcomes, just as a caseworker would in an individual case. You will have an ability to work effectively with individuals, groups, agencies and external authorities. You know how to manage conflict by striving for accepted solutions and you will hang onto those values of equity, fairness, social justice and a commitment to the service user.

Therefore, armed with these competencies, you can take comfort that you are not approaching the management task empty handed and you will, in fact, be able to draw on a range of professional competencies that will assist you as you develop more generic management skills. However, as you move into your new role, it is worth acknowledging that this transformation from practice to management represents a big personal change. A significant part of this transition is the letting go of your previous role and the acceptance of the new reality and challenges (Scragg, 2001). You will have to learn the language and the norms of management, and realise that there will be different expectations placed upon you (Scragg, 2001).

Management skills

A successful manager combines a number of management skills, personal traits and values, none of which will be alien to you. The following list is a common sense synopsis of what makes a good manager (Hannaway and Hunt, 1995):

- Being productive: getting things done.
- Setting challenging goals for oneself.
- Fluency in expressing ideas.
- Being an assertive communicator.
- Technical competence.
- Team leading skills.
- Being loyal and supportive to management and colleagues.
- Having a positive approach to problems.
- Being prepared to make sacrifices for your career.
- Having a personal meaning in life.

These are generic characteristics that are as applicable to the social care manager as they are to the commercial manager. Most of them do not have to be learned, but they do have to be practised if they are to become second nature.

Assumptions and myths

Assumptions

There are a number of assumptions that people hold when they come fresh into management (Sayles, 1979):

- The objectives will be clear.
- Results will be quick to appear, and clearly associated with inputs of effort.
- There will be plenty of time for analysis and decision making.
- Subordinates will respect and respond.
- Planning is important so there will be plenty of time for it.
- Means and ends will be clearly defined and there will be no contradictions or inconsistencies.
- Getting promoted will mean fewer people messing around with your decisions.
- The resources made available will be equal to the task assigned.
- People will be given the necessary authority to carry out their assignments.

Unfortunately, the reality is not like this and you are going to have to hit the ground running in a fairly messy environment.

Myths

When it comes to the specifics of managing social care it has been argued that a number of myths prevail (Weinbach, 1994):

- *Management is only the work of managers.* This provokes an adversarial, 'us and them' relationship. In reality management is everyone's work. Caseworkers manage individual cases, caseloads and their day. The basic function of organising can be performed at any level.
- *Management has little effect on services.* This supposes that direct service workers can insulate themselves from managers when, in fact, management and services are interdependent. Management decisions at all levels can support or jeopardise the delivery of effective services. Social care managers operate from the same value base as practitioners.

- *Management is just a technical skill.* This makes a false assumption about the values and professional identity of managers. In reality management requires much more than just technical skill. It also requires significant people skills, political know-how and professional principles.
- *Management is just the application of practice skills.* This assumes that management is only a people skill where staff can be viewed as clients. However, while the management of social care places a high premium on relationships and interpersonal skills, it also draws on other areas such as organisational theory and business.

The essence of management is specific functions performed with the intention to promote productivity and organisational goal attainment. The essential task of the social care manager is to build an optimal work environment conducive to effective delivery of services to the client. It is a proactive role that requires additional perspectives over and above what is required in direct practice. Without management in social care, staff and clients might turn up when they felt like it, staff could do whatever they felt like, there would be no guidelines or standards, there would be no sense of the agency's role in the community, no identifiable leader and no means of helping staff upgrade their skills and knowledge. Therefore, the manager's role is to do the planning, staffing, organising, controlling and leading.

Short term goals

Armed with the knowledge that you are not entirely a fish out of water as you take up a management position, set yourself some immediate goals that will help you establish yourself:

- Orientate yourself.
- Get to know your boss.
- Get to know your team.
- Make plans for the future.

Orientate yourself

You could decide to stay in your office and read every scrap of paper until you are 'bomb-proof' and able to answer any question that is thrown at you. However, the difficulty with this approach is that it is like not taking the car out onto the road until you have passed the driving test (Lawrence, 1986). Besides, everything you need to know is not contained in a file. So get about in the first few days, meeting as many people as possible. It is a good way to discover what is really going on. You will not have to worry about seeking opinions; they will be as plentiful as bugs on a bumper. Make a habit of getting out and about regularly. It debunks the stereotype of the remote manager.

Every organisation has its own unique culture, and by mingling at all levels you will begin to get a feel for it. Staff often see the appointment of a new manager as an opportunity for change; that is to say, an opportunity for them to change things that they did not like in the old regime. Therefore it is important not to let the tail wag the dog. Have a good look around before you initiate any change. By all means take counsel from experienced staff, hear their ideas, but do not be drawn into making sudden changes that you might regret later. The primary objective at this early stage is to listen.

It is worth reflecting a little on how you want to come across, without making a theoretical performance of it. You know what they say; you never get a second chance to make a good first impression. So, be charming. No one wants to see a po-faced bore moping around the place. During this early period you are laying down the foundations of your future identity and credibility. Project a positive, confident attitude, even if you are not feeling one hundred per cent. If you act as if you are calm you will appear calm and, in time, you will become calm. Appearing confident does not mean that you have to know everything. Right now you are on a learning curve and you will not be expected to have all the answers.

Your boss

Your boss is probably the first person you are going to meet on the first day. They are in the best position to show you the ropes. It is important to be very clear from the beginning about what it is you are supposed to be doing. Therefore clarify your boss's expectations of you. If your boss is vague or ambiguous seek clarification because woolly instructions will lead to a woolly performance, for which you may be held accountable later. You would not let builders loose on your home without giving them clear instructions; likewise you need your riding instructions before you get going.

Find out what are the big issues on your boss's agenda. What matters the most? What are the threats and opportunities? The answers to these questions will provide an understanding between both of you as to the main things you are going to tackle first.

Establish what the reporting relationship is going to be and how frequently they want to see you. If there is not going to be regular contact, by what means does your boss want to be kept informed? Clarify how decisions get made and what scope you have for making decisions without prior approval.

It is very difficult to pass go if you do not have an open communication with your line manager. Therefore, it is worth investing a considerable effort in getting this right. Take a leaf out of the boy scouts' book and be prepared. Do your homework before you go in. Always be on time, listen and take notes. As far as possible anticipate work to be done and get on to it even before you are asked.

From the outset establish a set of objectives with your boss. Agree key result areas and clarify the standard of performance required. Agree goals that will help meet your objectives and set a date to review performance against those goals (Hannaway and Hunt, 1995).

If your boss has shortcomings they are likely to include:

- unclear objectives
- does not keep you informed
- makes decisions without consulting
- will not see you when it really matters
- no interest in your development
- indecisive
- does not represent your opinions
- consistently overloads you

Therefore, consciously manage your relationship with your boss as an integral part of your new role. To do this you must tune in to their wavelength and get to understand their view of the world. This may be a very different perspective to yours; but your objective is not to make friends, it is to develop a working relationship which does not necessarily involve liking someone. However, consistency in these areas will at least gain you their respect, and may help to shift some of their shortcomings.

Remember, your appointment represents a change for your boss as well. Allow a little time for things to gel. Seek feedback sooner rather than later. Things are more malleable in the early days when it is easier to make little adjustments before things get set in their ways.

Find out from your boss who else you should meet as part of your induction, both within the organisation and in the wider environment. If you have peers, such as managers of equal rank, you have a very valuable source of support. If not, identify the nearest approximation because peer support is important. Find out what is important to them and how things get done.

As the weeks go by only bring the big issues to your boss; that is why they get paid the big bucks. Sort the other stuff out yourself, that is what you get paid for now. But keep the boss informed. Bosses do not like surprises so it is important to keep them in touch with developments. It is much better to be accused of overloading with information than of failing to inform.

Bosses are very busy people, probably with a lot of other people competing for their time, and you will never see them sufficiently often for your satisfaction. It is a fact of life that when you want to see the boss about something you will receive one solution but you will also pick up two or three new tasks. Therefore, think twice before knocking on their door. If you manage to contain your anxiety and only trouble your boss with the heavy stuff you are much more likely to be given an audience. A closed door usually confronts the person who has worn a path to their boss's office.

The following list provides a summary of how to get along with your boss (Hannaway and Hunt, 1995):

- Aim for a good relationship.
- Be loyal.
- Bring your boss solutions, not problems.
- Meet deadlines.
- Keep your boss informed.
- When your boss makes a mistake do not rub it in.
- Do not be defensive: accept ideas or amendments.
- Never provoke confrontation in the presence of others.

- Time your approach to suit your boss's mood.
- Check precise terms of reference for each project.
- Help your boss to succeed.

Your team

Whether your staff group comprises one or one hundred it is, without exception, your biggest resource. They are the people that actually do the work, so it is in your own interest to mind them. Management is all about getting the job done through other people. On day one most of them will not be too conspicuous but, like the Bogeyman, they are out there. Your appointment means a lot to them as well as to you. It represents a significant change and, as you will learn, change needs to be managed. Maybe, they will be delighted at your arrival because they hated the last boss. Maybe they will hate your arrival because they loved the last boss. Either way, you have arrived and things are not going to be the same again.

See the staff as a group first. It is a bit daunting but well worth it. If you are nervous tell them so; it will endear you to them! Acknowledge that the arrival of a new manager can be unsettling and assure them that you are not going to rush in any sweeping changes. Fill them in on your background and experience to date; but there is no obligation on you to be personal. Get people to introduce themselves and to describe their role on the team and where that fits into the overall objectives of the organisation.

Talk in general terms about your hopes and ambitions and assure them that you will value their input. Find out what the majority identify as the big issues, and take note of the different positions if there is a difference of opinion. Ask their opinion as to what objectives you should set yourself in the first few weeks and what they consider to be the highest priorities for the team.

Think of the staff group in business terms as a going concern. Some things will be going well and some things will not. Any staff group is like a community; some people get along, some do not. Someone is going to have personal problems and someone else is going to be trouble. All human life is there. You can take it as a given that not everyone will like you. Do not take this personally; it is not a popularity contest. The most flattering thing a boss can be called is fair; nice is a bonus.

As part of the first team meetings ask individuals to brief you on their particular work. As well as providing you with helpful information for your induction, it also spreads responsibility for the content and business of the meetings. Team meetings should not be a solo performance.

Set the tone for future meetings by making a time for the next one and seeking some pertinent items for the agenda. Indicate some of the ground rules. Set out what you see the team meetings as providing. They provide you with an opportunity to give updates from the higher echelons of the organisation and the outside world; they provide a forum to brainstorm issues in advance of making decisions and for team members to generally update each other on what is going on in their area of responsibility.

After the group meeting see individual members of staff in turn over the next few weeks, and at your own pace. Restrict formal sessions to those who report directly to you, but try to get acquainted with everyone. As with the team meeting, allow each individual to express their views as to what the main issues are, both for the team and for them personally. Clarify their particular role; what they think is going well and what needs to be improved. Identify key challenges from each individual's perspective. Enquire into what their expectation is of you and how they would like to work with you. Finally, establish what long-term goals they would like to set for the team in the future.

As you see people do not make too many promises until you find your feet, but deliver on any commitments you do make. Your credibility is one of your biggest assets. It will take a few laps of the track before you can earn their trust, and at the moment you are only warming up.

In the beginning it can be difficult to assume a position of authority over someone who is perhaps more experienced than you, or older. If at first you are awkward with this allow yourself a little time to adjust to your newly acquired authority. Try it out, get used to it but do not under any circumstances avoid it. You have been entrusted with a position of leadership and authority comes with the territory.

Do not adopt an open door policy; otherwise you will be at everyone's beck and call. It is supposed to be the other way around! If you agree to see your key staff at appropriate intervals they should, in normal circumstances, be able to manage their anxieties in the intervening period. That is not to say you should be aloof, but a little bit of protection will ensure that you manage your time in accordance with your priorities.

Make plans for the future

The first couple of weeks are best spent on getting to know people and getting a sense of what the priority issues are. After this period of observation, set out your stall and start to make things happen (Adair, 2003). You are ready to begin making some objectives and establishing your priorities.

Your overall task is to co-ordinate the resources at your disposal in order to apply the maximum benefit to the client. Prioritise the tasks that you have to do. Spend time on the most important things, not just the tasks that you are good at or prefer. Do not do what someone else can do for you, but do the things that only you can do. Many new managers make the fatal mistake of continuing to be caseworkers, behaving like some sort of super trouble-shooter. It is one thing to provide advice and guidance when asked, it is quite another do someone else's job for them. Such behaviour undermines and irritates staff; so do not fall into that trap. Instead concentrate on taking a more strategic approach.

In overall terms you are assuming responsibility for the work of your team, its performance, standards and future direction. It will take time to familiarise yourself with new business processes and with new people. It will also take time to establish yourself and to earn the trust of others below, above and beside you.

From the outset you will be confronted by all this busyness; a group of individuals franticly doing their own thing. Social care is notorious for dealing with individual cases without looking at the bigger picture. For example, I have seldom come across a social care team that sets annual objectives, either for individuals or for the team as a whole. They are much more likely to be running around saving the world on a case-by-case basis. Staff tend to get caught up in their individual cases and lose sight of the overall strategic direction of the team or the organisation.

As manager it is your job to convert all this busyness into a business. So, consider where it is you want to go first. Consider too what new skills you need to develop in order to get you there. In an ideal world an external mentor is a great resource to a new manager; someone who knows the business but is not caught up in the day to day politics of your organisation, and can provide coaching from a safe distance. Either way, begin to put together a vision for the future. Confer with your team as you clarify the direction you want to go in, and then set off. You are on the road to managing social care!

Main messages

- You are the boss now so start getting used to it.
- Be yourself.
- Your social care competencies and values come with you into management.
- Get around in the first few weeks (don't hide!)
- Clarify your boss's expectation of you from the start.
- Think of your team as a going concern.

Chapter 2

Managing the Service

If you don't know where you are goin', you will probably not wind up there.

Forrest Gump

Managing in human service organisations

Once you have found your feet after the first few weeks, the next step is to establish where are you going and how are you going to get there.

When I started out as a young social worker nobody told me what the business of the department actually was. I was like someone with amnesia hopping on a bus, not knowing where it had come from or where it was going. Providing social services is a bit like that; they are circular in nature with no clean-cut beginning, middle and end. An intervention may be over a prolonged period of time. For example, a care of older people team may spend years maintaining older people at home and in their own community. It is often demand-led; the business comes to you, often in overwhelming amounts. Unlike commercial businesses you do not have to market a product. It is more a case of managing the referrals that come to you in an unsolicited manner. This in itself can be a cause of some confusion because there is not always clarity about what service is provided, in what measure, who should receive it, what standards apply or how effectiveness is measured. This muddle is not necessarily the fault of the service provider, rather it is reflective of the nature of the business, which is complex and longitudinal in nature.

Generally speaking social care workers are not great at planning from month to month or year to year. They tend to deal with whatever lands on their lap, in terms of individuals or caseloads, without taking into account the bigger picture. However, as a manager, it is necessary to take a more global view of where you are and where you are heading and to add some method to the madness of your team's hectic routine. This starts with developing an appreciation of the environment within which you are working.

The working environment

The typical business environment has customers, suppliers and competitors. The motivation to make a profit ensures that efficiency is high on the agenda. In human service organisations, however, efficiency must be balanced against equity which must address professional obligations to the client and, therefore, cannot over emphasise efficiencies, such as cost savings, at the client's expense.

In business the loyalty of the customer is prized because loyal customers come back time and again. Ideally customers are rendered dependant on a particular product or service so that they have to come back for more. Conversely, in social care long term dependency would be seen as an indication of failure, since one of its core values is to help people to help themselves.

In social care, too, there are no real competitors. There may be some competition for funding sources, but human services are not going to fight over clients. Unlike business, where a lot of energy is spent on gaining the advantage, it has been suggested that a social care service would be only too pleased if another service came along to share some of the clients (Weinbach, 1994).

Whether they are in the statutory or non-governmental side, your staff, having chosen a career in social care, will have fundamentally good intentions and a desire to make a difference. However, there are cultural issues unique to both that need to be identified and addressed at an early stage.

Voluntary organisations are much more likely to be united in a common cause. They are usually focused on a single social issue such as homelessness, older people or a particular disability. The hallmark of a voluntary organisation is that it should be independent of state control and free to independently advocate its cause. This independence must not be compromised, even when a voluntary organisation is in receipt of state funding. It is better to be accused of biting the hand that feeds you than to be accused of being ambiguous about altruism.

In statutory organisations the cause is more likely to be blurred with various professional groupings holding onto their own values and ethics. These will concern social justice, advocacy, equity and a commitment to the user. This is often evidenced in large, complex, organisations that have a variety of professionals at the operational level, but who are managed at a senior level by non-professionals. Professionals often view this layer as administrators rather than directors of the service. In such situations professional autonomy may not sit well with corporate values. There is in effect a clash of loyalty between the service and the professions.

Within social care sectors generally there is a wariness that professional judgement might be stifled by too many control mechanisms, such as procedures and regulations. Social care workers are used to making their own minds up when it comes to decision-making, and they do not take kindly to external controls. These are strong cultural norms that you are not going to change over night, but it is best to walk into this milieu on day one with your eyes wide open. This is your working environment.

A human service model of management

The social care manager must identify and develop an organisational theory that is applicable to human service organisations. Such services seek to change people in some way. In effect the client is the organisation's input, raw material and product. It has been asserted (Sarri and Hasenfield, 1978) that in a human service model of management there are a number of critical preconditions:

- Clearly articulated goals based on valid data.
- Enforcement of worker accountability for achieving results.
- Facilitation of staff behaviour and implication of activities that bring results.
- Implementation of objective methods of evaluation.
- Securing the necessary resources for ongoing activities.
- Facilitation of personal and professional growth.
- Simplification of bureaucratic procedures.
- Development of ongoing problem solving and change mechanisms.
- Goal orientated case management as a basic strategy.
- Creation of ongoing mechanisms for affecting sound inter-organisational relations.

A tall order perhaps, but at least it clarifies the task of the social care manager and provides a blueprint for action. Perhaps the most essential objective of a new social care manager, as alluded to in the above list, is to develop a clear sense of purpose and this starts by being really unambiguous about what services your organisation is mandated to provide.

Mandate

A mandate is an authorative requirement; in other words it is what you are supposed to be doing. Working in the statutory sector your ultimate mandate is set out in law and associated regulations. There will be statutes setting out what your organisation is obliged to do. Working in a health and social service setting, as I do, there is a whole range of legislation governing what is to be done, my personal favourite being the Rats and Mice (Destruction) Act 1919, which 'places a legal duty on the occupier of land where an infestation exists, or is suspected, to abate that infestation and to take steps to prevent its reoccurrence'. Familiarise yourself with the laws that are relevant to your service and convert them into tasks for your team. If you are in a private or not-for-profit organisation you are more likely to be focused on a single function, for example the care of older people. However, your mandate will, most likely, be influenced by your funding agencies for, as we all know, he who pays the piper calls the tune.

Underneath the legislative platform you can expect to find layers of national and, or, local policies and strategies. A **policy** is a plan, expressed in general terms that guide our thinking and our actions. A **strategy** is more a plan of action, committing resources to meet a set objective. Again, as with the legislation, familiarise yourself with the policies and strategies that are relevant to your service. This should be done as part of your induction and in association with your boss, your peers and your staff.

Underneath all the legislation, policy and strategy there is, or should be, **protocols**. A protocol is a step-by-step guide as to how to preceed in particular circumstances. It avoids you having to make things up as you go along, or each time you do the same thing. Your main activities should be governed by protocols, so if they are not already in place prepare them in conjunction with your staff.

Mission

Mission can be described as the service's identity and direction in terms of doing its very best for the people it serves. Nowadays it is usual for a service to have a **mission statement**. For example, when you check into a hotel it is not uncommon to find a mission statement, written in spidery italics, waiting for you on the table in your room. The mission statement is an all-encompassing declaration of the best we want to do.

By way of example, the following is the mission statement of the Salvation Army, which obviously reflects their Christian values:

> *The Salvation Army, an international movement, is an evangelical part of the universal Christian Church. Its message is based on the bible. Its ministry is motivated by the love of God. Its mission is to preach the gospel of Jesus Christ and to meet human needs in his name without discrimination.*
>
> (Salvation Army, 2006)

This statement is further distilled into their lovely slogan, 'A heart to God and a hand to man.'

Another global organisation, that is more humanist in nature, is the Ford Foundation which has the following mission statement:

> *The Ford Foundation is a resource for innovative people and institutions worldwide. Our goals are to:*
> * *Strengthen democratic values.*
> * *Reduce poverty and injustice.*
> * *Promote international co-operation.*
> * *Advance human achievement.*
>
> (Ford Foundation, 2006)

According to the management guru, Peter Drucker, the ultimate test of a mission statement is not its beauty but that it delivers the right action. It needs to be operational in focus, otherwise it is just good intentions. It is the job of the manager to turn the mission statement into specifics (Drucker, 1990).

Vision

Closely associated with the concept of mission is that of vision. Vision is not so much a description of an unknown future as it is a statement of the values underlying an effective organisation (Kenny, 2003). There needs to be a creative tension between present reality and your articulated vision. All good managers have a good vision. When all about them are loosing their heads they retain clarity about where they are going. It is so easy to start drowning in the business of everyday work, but a good manager keeps their eye on the horizon line and retains that vision of how things could be and how to get there.

Vision is also about defining objectives in practical terms. It needs to be articulated in a passionate way that it will ignite a spark of excitement in staff, instilling in them energy and an openness to new ideas. If you are managing a section or arm of an organisation it is important that the corporate vision is tailored to fit your particular circumstances. Any expression or statement of your vision should describe a desirable outcome in a way that conveys meaning and inspiration to others. The best examples are short and sweet, like this one from Barnardo's, New Zealand:

A society where children can grow up to be caring people and quality parents.

(Barnardo's, 2006)

The management process

Armed with these noble thoughts of where you want to go you can now take some time to consider the nuts and bolts of how you are going to get there. As a manager you will be involved in a range of activities, some of which are not actually exclusive to management, and will not be unfamiliar to you. However, how these activities are orchestrated *is* the management process, and how well you do it will determine how good you are at management. Depending on what book you read the activities vary, but they can all be boiled down to three basic elements, managing people, processes and information:

People	Processes	Information
motivating	organising	gathering
co-ordinating	planning	analysing
leading	doing	distributing
delegating	evaluating	forecasting

supervising	controlling	communicating
influencing	negotiating	generating
directing	budgeting	
	advocating	

Juggling these elements well is the art of good management: try three or more at one time and you will find out!

Organising is all about orchestrating the various elements, such as people, money, and tools to come together to accomplish a common goal. There are basically two levels of organisation; organising yourself and organising others. In terms of organising yourself time is a limited resource, so use it wisely. Some things are urgent, some things are important and some things are urgent and important. Learn to distinguish the difference between them.

Since management is about getting the job done through other people it is important that you influence how they are organised. Your staff will determine your success as a manager. Ensure they are performing the tasks that will contribute to the right outcome. Like a conductor of an orchestra, you need to bring people together who perform different, but interconnected, tasks. You must lead from the front, control the timing and blend the action into a harmonious experience

Control is about keeping things on track so that objectives will be delivered. Depending on your position in the line management this can be done through directing individuals, or groups of individuals, towards the completion of objectives. It is about regulating the work on the way in, reviewing it on the way through, and evaluating it on the way out.

Negotiating is a bread and butter task of a manager. It is multi-faceted, potentially involving employees, employers, peers, staff representatives, funding agencies and other stakeholders. At whatever level it occurs it involves a process that dates back to the time of Methuselah; the art of give and take.

Service planning

By their nature social service teams do not always work to an explicit plan. As alluded to earlier they tend to take tasks, one at a time, and just get on with it in a bull-headed manner without ever looking up to see where they are headed, or without ever reviewing where they have come from. They are consumed with the business of the day, which, let's face it, is often very demanding and emotionally draining.

To run a successful business you need a plan. Service planning is about making strategic vision a reality; identifying the tasks that need to be undertaken, and then allocating them into particular organisational functions. Therefore, rather than jumping in the deep end, it is essential, once you have orientated yourself within the organisation, that you spend some quality time setting short term and medium objectives for you service.

Although there is relatively little written about social service management specifically there has been a significant growth in the literature relating to health service management. Many of the principles of health service management can be applied to social services with far more relevance than commercial management.

The individual elements of a service plan are like stepping-stones to a successful outcome. Step over them in a sequential manner and you will arrive at your destination without getting your feet wet. A service plan can be defined as a document that provides an overview of services to be provided, within a particular time frame and within existing financial constraints. Whereas a strategic plan has longer-term objectives a business plan should be seen as an annual event. It is about taking stock of how we are achieving strategic actions.

The key elements of a service plan are as follows:

- mission/vision
- achievements over the past year
- strategic direction
- key priorities for the coming year
- objectives and targets
- arrangements for monitoring and evaluation

By now you know about mission and vision. **Achievements** over the past year can take the form of a short review of the current position of your service against objectives set out last year. It is an ideal opportunity to engage your staff in the planning process. Facilitate them to answer some basic questions, such as:

- How did we do?
- What did we do well?

- Where did we not meet targets?
- What were the difficulties in achieving success?

Emphasis should be placed on the service as a whole, not just new service developments. Any achievements expressed should reflect the objectives set out for the previous year. As a new manager you will not necessarily know what happened last year so it is a good way of finding out from your staff. If, as well might be the case, your team did not have a written service plan last year, panic not. Get them to tell you in their own words what they where trying to achieve and how they went about trying to achieve it. What were the banana skins and what were the lucky breaks? Then write it all down.

If you hold a budget you will need to set out your financial position. If you do not have a budget you still need to have some regard as to where the money comes from and where it goes. For a start, the chances are your staff is your organisation's biggest expense. Is there anything, from a human resource perspective, that could be improved upon in the coming year? Do you sign people's travelling expenses or subsistence claims? Are there courier, taxi or transport expenses? Do you purchase products or services for, or on behalf of, your team? Anything that costs money, including staff, needs to be considered in terms of value for money, just like you do when you are doing your household shopping, so make sure the money is well spent.

In reporting on achievements over the previous year you need to consider any trends in activity, and for this you need a yard stick; something to measure the activity against. For example, it could be expressed in terms of greater throughput of patients in the convalescent home, a reduction in the number of children coming into care, less admissions to the psychiatric hospital through increased home-based support. In other words talk in terms of percentage increases or decreases in the level of service activity.

Your **strategic direction** is the longer-term objective of your organisation to achieve its mission and vision. So what are you going to do next year to advance this cause? Like a mouse with a big block of cheese you need to do a little nibbling. Bite off a bit of your organisation's strategic plan and convert it into tasks for your team in the coming year. In so doing you need to ask yourself, what are the strategic issues that need to be addressed this year?

In setting **key priorities** for the coming year you should link them also to the bigger picture. By doing this you are linking long term goals with what is achievable in the year. Do not limit your priorities to new service developments, but to your service as a whole. Consider what the likely challenges are going to be, and what resources are available to you. Next you need to establish tasks to get things done.

Objectives should be crystal clear and specific. This is not the lofty stuff of mission statements, such as aspiring to improve social gain; this is the nitty gritty of exactly what is going to be done, by whom, when and at what cost. Objectives need to be realistic, tangible tasks that are achievable within a stipulated time frame. For example:

The number of teenagers using the youth club will increase by 20% within the next twelve months.

or

Waiting times for our counselling service will not exceed one month throughout the coming year.

It is advisable not to be over ambitious in setting objectives, as it looks bad at the end of the year if many of them have not been achieved. It is better to lower the bar than to miss the jump. However, even with the best-laid plans sometimes you will not achieve your objective. Things can change. If you do not achieve an objective it needs to be reported on anyhow, and set out what you are going to do about it in the year to come.

Objectives need to add value, not only to your own area of work, but also to the corporate objectives of your organisation as a whole. They can be long term or short term. In any event, involve your team in identifying them, carrying them out and reviewing them. Remember to distinguish between objectives and activities; you want to measure what you achieve, not what you do.

Targets (or goals) should be SMART objectives that clearly set out what is to be done, by when and by how much:

- Specific
- Measurable
- Achievable
- Realistic
- Time bound

Lastly, put in place a system for **monitoring** your service plan. It should be a benchmark by which you can monitor your achievements against what is in the service plan.

Monitoring is a way of assessing the effectiveness, appropriateness and efficiency of each of the constituent parts of your service as a whole. If objectives are a starting point and outcomes are a destination, then monitoring is a set of milestones along the way. As you walk the road take out your map occasionally and identify where you are. If you have strayed, make adjustments. You need to consider issues of quality as well as quantity and cost. One straightforward way of gauging the effectiveness of your service is to ask the service users what they think. Assessing customer satisfaction should be a central part of the monitoring process.

Generally speaking it is notoriously difficult to measure the effectiveness of social services. Because of the nature of the business there is no certainty as to what a desirable outcome might be and, therefore, it can be hard to find reliable ways of measuring such outcomes (Kenefick, 1998). In setting **performance indicators** for social services most people stick to quantifiable data, such as the number of older people awaiting residential care. Also measuring quality outcomes can be tricky. For example, if a service for an older person finds a lovely residential facility in gig-time, and it is affordable and within the person's locality you still may score a zero in customer satisfaction if the person does not want to be there in the first place. Therefore, consider carefully the outcome you want to measure.

The following checklist provides a synopsis of what needs to be captured in a service plan:

- The purpose of the service.
- The vision of the future of the service.
- The broad aims and objectives.
- The service offered and to whom.
- Any intended changes to the service.
- Short-term targets for activity levels and outcomes.
- Targets for income and expenditure.
- How to keep in touch with the needs and expectations of service users.
- How you are going to address quality and standards.

In short the service plan needs to answer three simple questions:

1. What are we trying to do?
2. What is the best way of doing it?
3. What resources are we going to need?

Controlling intake

One of the most important functions a social care manager will have to perform is the control of intake. I have never come across a social care team of any description that did not describe itself as over worked. There is no doubt that social care is a demand-led service with no shortage of customers, often presenting in overwhelming numbers. Some services are more protected than others. For example, a day care centre for adults with a learning disability might have a capacity for, say, sixty people. There may well be pressure because of mounting waiting lists and so on, but it is still possible to hold the line by refusing to take in any more clients. In effect, the people on the waiting list are someone else's problem and the centre's duty of care is to the sixty people on the inside. On the other hand, a statutory social work team engaged in child protection work may have an equally full workload but there is still a moral expectation that children requiring immediate care and protection will receive it. Similarly, you cannot put house fires on a waiting list. Therefore, it becomes evident that the control of intake should be a priority task for managers where the service does not have the opportunity to operate a quota system. This involves issues such as assessment, eligibility and prioritisation.

The very thought of controlling intake means, in effect, that you are trying to prevent someone from receiving a service; otherwise you would take everything that came in the door. Therefore two cautionary notes need to be sounded. The first is to be very clear about the business you are in. Social services have, in general, been criticised for not having a clear idea of precisely what services are provided, who might avail of them, to what standard and in what measure they are delivered. It is a good idea to write a statement of purpose for your service that encapsulates in a nutshell what it is that you do. For example:

This children's home provides residential care to boys and girls aged between 10 and 14 years who have specific needs that cannot be met within their own family or community.

The other point is not to lose sight of the fact that you are in a car profession in which the consumer should come first. By way of illustration, I once knew a social work team that received a call to say a little child was begging at the foot of a pedestrian bridge over a river in the city centre. The day was cold, wet and windy and the child was miserable. One side of the bridge was the social workers' catchment area; the other side was in another team's area. Guess what the first question the social worker asked? 'Which side of the bridge is he on?' That question ended up being exposed on a chat show on national radio where, needless to say, our service got its teeth kicked in. The moral of the story is that services should be needs-led not service driven.

The process of controlling intake might well start with a clever little question I heard somewhere: 'Why us now?' The fact of the matter is that to be able to say no to something you first have to know what to say yes to.

Needs assessment

There are a number of reasons for conducting assessments which might include (Soriano, 1995):

- Justification for funding.
- Regulation or laws that mandate needs assessment.
- Resource allocation and decision making – determining the best use of limited resources.
- Assessing the needs of specific, underserved, sub-populations.
- As part of programme evaluations.

Essentially, assessment is about identifying the current situation, identifying the desired situation and measuring the gap, which is the need. The assessment of need:

- Identifies how best to deploy resources.
- Matches needs to services.
- Increases accountability.
- Puts the customer centre stage.

As manager your primary concern should be that everyone is using the same yardstick to measure need. Many assessment tools have been devised

vices, and you may well find that national or organisational
in place for your particular service. However, in general
I need to create a checklist for staff from which they can
s to assessed need. The bottom line is who needs the service

Risk assessment

A common concept nowadays is that of risk assessment; that is to say a specific means of identifying risk factors. It is a particularly helpful tool at the point of entry to the service. A determination can be made as to indicators present which are harmful to the client, or could be if an intervention is not made. Risk assessment can form part of the overall assessment, or it can stand alone as a tool in its own right. If your service does not already have one, you are well advised to draw up your own list of **risk indicators**. The following are good examples that were devised by Social Information Systems Ltd.:

Examples of generic risk indicators

1. Breakdown of support network – carer, welfare system from work etc., resulting in the person not being able to meet their needs themselves. This might also include traumatic life events (bereavement, hospital admission) isolation affecting the ability to self-care, or homelessness or the threat of eviction.
2. Permanent and substantial or acute disability – physical or mental.
3. Substantial or sudden deterioration in physical or mental health.
4. Inability to maintain personal care (hygiene, safety, nutrition).
5. Risk of self-harm, suicide or severe self-neglect.
6. Risk of exploitation (sexual, financial).
7. Vulnerability to drugs, alcohol.
8. Severe levels of challenging behaviour (aggression, antisocial behaviour, abusiveness, hazardous behaviour).
9. Significant communication needs.
10. Refusing essential services.

Social Information Systems Ltd., 2005

Examples of risk indicators relating to adults

Previous contact

1. Prior substantiated abuse or allegations of exploitation (e.g. financial, sexual).
2. Prior unsubstantiated abuse or allegations of exploitation.
3. Escalating pattern of contact with social work department.

Client factors

4. Intellectual or social development impaired or deteriorated.
   - Intellectual disability.
   - Impaired cognitive skills for daily decision-making (including dementia and loss of memory).
   - No stable day programme (employment, learning, leisure, hobbies, ability to organise day).
5. Medical care issues, e.g.
   - Substantial or sudden deterioration in health.
   - Emotional or mental health concern (including self-harm, impact of traumatic life events, motivation, depression/anxiety/mood, sleeping patterns).
   - Physical health concern (including terminal or life-threatening illness, mobility, balance, eating, drinking, swallowing, medication use and ability to self-medicate, continence, tissue viability, need for specialist equipment or support).
   - Sexual health concern.
   - Substance misuse concern.
6. Communication or sensory difficulties.
7. Relationships, attachments, affections and resilience e.g.
   - Poor attachment to family members and significant others.
   - Severe levels of challenging behaviour (aggression, antisocial behaviour, offending behaviour, abusiveness, hazardous behaviour) or recent significant behaviour change.
   - Victim or perpetrator of bullying or discrimination.
8. Inappropriate or poor self-care, independence, autonomy, isolation e.g.
   - Problems with washing or grooming, bathing, dressing, undressing, night-time needs.

- Unable to perform basic domestic tasks (e.g. housework, food preparation, cooking, shopping, laundry).
9. Significant identity issues.
10. Client is from ethnic minority community.
11. Supervision and safety issues, e.g.
    - Lack of safety in home environment.
    - Orientation or wandering.
    - History of falls.
    - Possible risk to others.

Partner or carer capacity
12. Sudden breakdown in care network.
13. Client lives alone.
14. Main carer is aged under 18 or over 70 years.
15. Partner or carer has alcohol or drugs issues.
16. Partner or carer has emotional or mental health issues.
17. Partner or carer has a disability (including intellectual disability).
18. Partner or carer has other physical health issues.
19. Partner or carer has communication or sensory difficulties.
20. Partner or carer has a history of causing serious harm to adults or children.
21. Partner or carer has a history of aggressive or challenging behaviour (including domestic violence, offending behaviour, power or control issues).
22. Partner or carer has poor caring skills.
23. Partner or carer is struggling to cope.

Extended family and community factors
24. Family socially isolated.
25. Extended family is over-protective.
26. Absence of facilities or equipment in home or community.
27. Lack of access to suitable transport.
28. Housing difficulties (including poor amenities, access, heating, temporary accommodation, homelessness, threat of homelessness, hazardous environment, frequent moves in accommodation, overcrowding, need for adaptation to meet client's specific needs).

29. Dependence on benefits or state assistance.
30. Resource or financial management problems.
31. Family experience or fear of crime or antisocial behaviour.
32. No other agency support.
33. Refusing essential services.
34. Closure or disengagement from support network or social services.

Customise a set of risk indicators for your service. It is a valuable, standardised, yardstick that can be used during initial assessment or as part of a case review.

Eligibility criteria

Bearing in mind that services should be needs led there are two cautionary tales to be told when it comes to eligibility criteria. Firstly, I remember visiting a social service department in a local authority in London, in search of new ideas. They boasted that they did not have a waiting list. This intrigued me, as it was a busy inner city office with plenty of poverty, deprivation and social need. However, when I scratched the surface it became obvious that they had raised the bar so high that only a minority could get over it. Although eligibility criteria is good for controlling intake it can also have the negative side effect of excluding people who could genuinely benefit from the service. In such situations moderate need tends to get ignored and the benefits of early intervention are lost. In the long term this is not good as there is a real risk that this will generate more acute need. It is the social care equivalent of parking the ambulance at the bottom of the cliff.

Secondly, eligibility criteria came in for some very stern criticism in England following the death of a young girl from prolonged, undetected and sadly fatal child abuse. The author of an inquiry report, Lord Laming, had such forceful and sobering comments to make that they are worth reproducing here:

The management of the social care of children and families represents one of the most difficult challenges for local government. The variety and range of referrals, together with the degree or risk and urgency, needs strong leadership, effective decision-making, reliable record keeping, and a regular review of performance. Sadly many of those from social services who gave evidence seemed to spend a lot of time and energy devising ways of limiting access to services, and adopting mechanisms designed to reduce service demand.

(Laming Enquiry, 2003: 1.52)

He went on to conclude:

Little I heard in this inquiry convinced me that local authorities accept that in public service, the needs of the public must come first.

(Laming Enquiry, 2003: 1.54)

Therefore it is clear that eligibility criteria should not be used as a self-serving mechanism for the organisation. However, used responsibly it can provide clarification for service users, and the public at large, by determining who may avail of which services. This in turn allows managers to undertake effective assessments and match services to assessed needs. An example of eligibility criteria might look like this:

Our services for adults include:
- *People over 65 years.*
- *Adults with a learning disability.*
- *Adults with a chronic illness.*
- *Adults with a physical or sensory disability.*

Prioritisation

Risk indicators and eligibility criteria may be further categorised into high, moderate and low risk so that priority can be given to cases that require help the most. It is also a way of deciding who gets the service now, and who has to wait. It is important to put a system in place, which ensures that all open cases in the system are more pressing than those on the waiting list.

Workload management

One way of controlling the overall pattern of work in the team, once it passes intake, is to introduce a workload management system. Workload management looks beyond the worker/client interaction and considers all aspects of the work being undertaken. It considers indirect work such as meetings, travel, recording, administration and so on. Each individual accounts for their time, usually on a prepared form. In this way patterns emerge that show what individuals are doing with their time. The worker can estimate the amount of time particular tasks will take, thus optimising time and resources.

Obviously this approach has benefits for staff supervision, but the aggraded information allows you to look at overall team activity. In this way it enables you to make any adjustments required in the overall work of the team. For example:

Team log

	Direct contact	Meetings	Admin	Phone	Travel	Duty	Supervision	Leave	Total time
Worker 1									
Worker 2									
Worker 3									

Social Information Systems Ltd, 2005

Workload management should not be confused with caseload weighting. The latter apportions a weighting value to individual cases, depending on their severity and complexity. It is a very restrictive system which focuses on what work cannot be taken on, rather than on what can be done within the existing workload.

Managing within available resources

In a demand-led business there will never be enough resources. The eternal cry of the social care worker is 'we don't have enough resources!' If I had a cent for every time I heard that mantra I would be able to eliminate national debt. The primary resources that managers have at their disposal are people, money and information. The skill is to manage as best you can within the resources available to you. This requires an ongoing balancing act between need and demand on one side and availability of services on the other. Take responsibility for service delivery from the outset. Be as creative and as inventive as you can. Do not settle for binary thinking;

rather generate lots of options. Some of the best managers I ever saw were poor people on tight budgets who could demonstrate infinite inventiveness in the way they could make the last few bob go further.

It is important for the manager to convey to staff that their task is to do the best they can with what they have got. It is all too easy for staff groups to become disempowered and disenchanted and to start whining about management, the government and so on. They are not being asked to do the impossible, only the best they can. By you assuming overall responsibility for service delivery you are absolving staff of that particular worry.

The essential task here is to hitch your staff group up to the overall mission of the organisation; to discourage an 'us and them' mentality and to encourage a 'we are us' mentality. Telling social care workers to do it because you are the boss will not get you very far. Leading them towards professional excellence does. It is important therefore to demonstrate a strong personal commitment to the needs of the client and to focus staff energy on doing their best with what they have. In this way the service will be operating at its optimum level.

Measuring performance

Teams will perform to their optimum when members know exactly what is required of them. A good performance will be greatly facilitated by having clear objectives, and these need to be clearly understood by the team. Therefore there is an opportunity here to gel the team by linking them together towards a common end. That shared purpose is the key to good teamwork. There is no point in setting objectives if you do not have a way of measuring results; therefore, measuring performance is all about developing a yardstick to measure how you are doing. Its purpose is to:

- Promote effectiveness and improvements in service delivery.
- Optimise performance by establishing what needs to be done to improve results.
- Improve customer satisfaction and overall accountability to the user, funding agencies and general public.
- Match progress against national priorities and strategic objectives.

It is not easy to measure effectiveness in social services because there is not always clarity about what constitutes a desirable outcome. That is why it is so important to clarify at the outset exactly what it is you are trying to achieve. However, it is by no means impossible to develop **performance indicators** to measure success. Here are a few examples:

Objective: To promote self-sufficiency among adults with a learning disability living in supported accommodation.

Performance indicator: All clients working in open employment settings.

Objective: To enhance the experience and opportunities for children in residential care.

Performance indicator: All children in residential care have an up to date care plan and allocated key worker.

There are a number of key areas in which performance can be effectively measured. For example, indicators of **appropriateness** can be effectively measured in care settings against what is considered to be best practice. Hence, the rate of transfer of in-patients in the mental health service back to the community, where treatment is more appropriate, can be accurately measured. Indicators of **effectiveness** can be measured in terms of success. For example, it could be increased uptake in the number of foster parents recruited or the number of attendees at a counselling centre. Examples of **efficiency** might include the number of care centres inspected in a set period, or the waiting time between an application to adopt and the commencement of the assessment (Butler, 2000).

Performance indicators tend to be used to measure quantifiable data, such as attendances, discharges and so on. However, it is not impossible to link PIs to **quality**. For example, indicators of effectiveness, such as increased uptake of a service, can be stated in terms of a quality initiative. Indicators of adverse quality can also be used, such as the number of complaints received or the number of re-admissions to care. Users' perceptions and experience of a service can also be used as a quality measure. Fair access to services in terms of meeting need, clear eligibility criteria and information on the service can be used as a quality measure.

By using such measures to monitor outcomes it is actually possible to establish what works best. Then resources can be connected to best results when budgets are being worked out. Nowadays, funding organisations look for clarity of purpose in a service, as well as clear expectations of outcomes. The extent to which an organisation can demonstrate cost effective and efficient services are important factors. Value for money is a big issue, particularly when times are tough. As a general rule the more money there is in the economy the less emphasis there is on control; but when the money dries up the squeeze is really on for cost effectiveness. Take post Beverage Britain for example. The original welfare state model that followed the Second World War gave way to some serious belt tightening in the oil crisis era of the 1970s. Accountability is always to the fore when money is scarce. In a riches to rags scenario the question shifts from 'What can you spend it on?' to 'What did you do with all the money we gave you?'

In order to monitor services against targets you are going to need information. The timely collection of data is important in this regard. You will need to practice your ability to analyse and interpret data and use it to improve performance

When setting objectives and establishing PIs they should be connected to national priorities and strategic objectives. Likewise, they should connect to the mission and purpose of the organisation. By measuring performance you are, in effect, **managing for results** in order to:

- Show a commitment to delivering an efficient and effective service.
- Justify decision-making.
- Attract investment by achieving favourable outcomes.
- Demonstrate the effectiveness and value of the service.
- Provide transparency and accountability to the user, funding authorities and the public.

Developing interventions that work best

Typically social care organisations apply 'casework' as a cure all for most ills. However, there is a growing realisation, particularly in the USA, that more targeted interventions are more likely to have the desired effect on particular problems. Hence, the concept of 'programme design' has emerged, involving the putting together of service combinations that have the best chance of a desirable outcome.

Designing a programme requires a number of sequential steps (Kettner, Moronrey and Martin, 1999):

1. *Defining programmes*: Some services will have clearly defined programmes in terms of staff, resources, clients and services to be

provided; others will be less well defined. If the latter is the case it will be necessary to itemise what amount of staff and other resources you propose to devote to each programme.

2. *Problem analysis*: Traditionally programmes were built in response to emotional appeals, (e.g. homeless children) rather than on a clear analysis of data as well as a good understanding of the nature of the problem. Therefore, it is essential to define the problem in terms of type, size and scope.

3. *Needs assessment*: There are four perspectives of need:
   - Normative need, as defined by a professional.
   - Perceived need, as seen by those experiencing it.
   - Expressed need , as evidenced by those who seek a service.
   - Relative need, the needs and resources in one geographic area compared to another.

   Accurately matching needs to services will follow from a good analysis of the problem. Identify how many in your area have this need and the sub-areas where the problems are most prevalent. Then get a handle on the volume of services that are required too address them.

4. *Selecting a strategy and establishing objectives*: There needs to be a strategy for reducing or eliminating the problem by meeting the need. Clarify what outcomes would be expected if the person received the service to be designed. Produce written objectives that specify the expected outcomes for clients.

5. *Programme design*: This is about putting the best possible package of services that will have the best chance of tackling the problem. In order to examine programme effectiveness results will need to be aggregated in terms of client access, service provision, service completion and outcome assessment. In other words, results need to be quantified and measured.

6. *Management information systems*: Whereas narrative case recording is useful for individual case analysis, the management of the overall programmes really requires a data base that can provide an aggraded picture of programme outcomes. Ideally this will require computerisation.

7. *Programme evaluation*: Evidence based programme planning provides information to staff on how well a programme performed against the stated objectives. It provides a means by which a manager can assess the amount of staff and other resources that were used and at what

cost. It also provides a clear means of evaluating outcomes for clients and possible ways to improve them.

Main messages

- Develop a clear sense of purpose and direction for your service: know where you are going.
- Prepare a written service plan to get you there.
- To say 'no' to a referral you must first clarify what you say 'yes' to.
- You will never have enough resources – manage what you've got well.
- Develop a yardstick to measure how your service is doing against its stated objectives.
- Put together interventions and service combinations that have the best chance of a desirable outcome for the client.

Chapter 3

Managing People

Under a good general there are no bad soldiers.

Chinese proverb

The frontier people who formed the wagon trains across North America in the early days came with little, but held onto a vision of a better future. They stuck together through thick and thin. They endured hardship, seeing it as a means to an end. They were not always sure exactly where they were, but they knew where they wanted to go. Uncertainty was a daily reality, so they had to be brave, and clever. So, taking a leaf out of the trailblazers' book you now need to hitch your team to the mission wagon. Excite them about where you want to bring them and get those wagons rolling!

Leadership

Leadership is all about getting the most out of people. People who are inspired make willing followers. People willingly follow leaders that can show fortitude in times of adversity. It is a huge morale booster for staff when the boss successfully takes the helm in troubled waters and steers them to a safe haven. Good leaders are heroes: you will never see a statue to commemorate a loser. Napoleon is reputed to have said: 'I fight with my soldiers' dreams'. This is a wonderful description of how to connect day to day operations to the overall vision and the mission of the organisation.

Professional values predominate in social care, where the client always comes first. As has been mentioned previously, social care workers, in particular situations can have a divided loyalty between their professional values and their employing organisation. For example, as advocates for their clients they will not be shy about highlighting a resource deficit to senior management.

Also, there is less value placed on hierarchal rule in social care, than in other human services. As a consequence social care teams tend to have flatter organisational structures, if not in rank, then at least in practice whereby decisions are inclined to be vested in the group as opposed to the leader of the group.

However, despite these professional traits, be under no illusion that you are in charge. Staff are entitled, of course, to contribute to decision-making but the final arbiter ought to be you, the manager. By tapping into their professional values you will find the raw material to lead them to a place that is right for the client and still need not be in conflict with the overall direction of the organisation. Leadership is the art of bringing people with you. I learned somewhere the concept that managers direct but leaders show the way. Bellowing instructions will neither bring you results or respect but leading from the front will bring you both. Therefore, the essential task of the manager as leader is, not only to lead the horse to water, but to make it drink as well. Leadership is all about securing employee commitment.

Leadership aptitudes are commonly explored as competency issues at interviews for new managers. A common question is, 'What is your leadership style?' Implicit in this question is a belief that each of us possesses an innate personality type that pre-determines the type of leader we will make, if at all. Wrong: leadership can be learned. True, many high profile leaders are strong, extrovert people with a kick-ass approach to achievement; but if being an authority figure does not come naturally to you, persevere and you will find that your confidence will grow. More important than natural assertiveness is the ability to communicate the mission to others in a way that excites them about the future.

Bear in mind also that a degree of power comes with the territory of being placed in a leadership position. You will not have to seek it; it will be bestowed upon you. However, like a wizard with a new wand, be careful how you use it! It has been suggested (Gilbert, 2005) that 'authority' is perhaps a more apt word because authority is carried by how we are perceived by others as an individual, through our personal and professional attributes, our experience and the job we have been asked to undertake. People are considered to be authoritative when they possess the personal and professional/managerial attributes that others wish to follow (Gilbert, 2005).

The team

The old adage goes 'There's good news and there's bad news. The bad news is that we're lost; the good news is that we're making great time!' It pays to know where you are going, especially when you are the leader. Effective teams agree upon their vision and mission, and then agree upon strategies to implement them on an individual and sub-group basis (Eales-White, 1996). Clarity of purpose is all-important, both in terms of the role of each individual and of the team as a unit. Setting goals will provide clarity of purpose. The key to good goal setting is old fashioned passion, where the team is collectively excited about where it is going. Mobilise them around their common objective and make sure each one of them is clear about their individual role in achieving the overall aims of the team and the organisation as a whole (Boyle, 1997). Alongside clear objectives there needs to be clear expectations of what outcomes there ought to be. Make certain that the team is crystal clear about what it is it is trying to achieve.

The essential difference between your team and one in business is that it is not motivated solely by profit. Therefore staff incentives have to come from other sources. By their nature social care workers are social activists and as such they want the best for the people they serve. They have a vocation. Harvest this idealism and you will have a well-motivated and effective team. Indications of a well-motivated team include:

- Being happy at work.
- Co-operative rather than competitive.
- Taking responsibility.
- Performing well.
- Delivering on time.
- Respect for management.

Bringing a bunch of individuals into the same room does not constitute a team. A team will not become a team until it agrees to be one. Members need to come to the realisation that they are inter-dependant and that team goals can best be achieved through mutual support. Teams bring about a sense of collective accountability. This is important as a team is not just a set of individuals, it is a group charged with performing complementary tasks to achieve a common end. Think of a football team. Each team member plays in a different position, but they play as a consolidated unit that is focused on the same desired outcome. This affiliation to others is an important element of team building; that sense of belonging combined with the knowledge that each team member is making their own unique contribution to the organisation as a whole.

Seek to create an environment where your relationship with staff is based on trust and support, where you are able to respond flexibly to their needs. The manager's understanding of staff needs and the relationship with them is one of the most important factors in the success of a team (Scragg, 2001).

To a large extent effective teams become self-managing (Eales-White, 1996). They know what is expected of them, know how to do it and they get on and do just that. However, as professionals they require a little space, so do not be afraid to give it to them. Keeping with the football analogy, you are the coach, directing, motivating and getting the most out of everyone. You cannot play the game for them, so you have to allow the team a degree of autonomy. Yet, on the other hand, this has to be balanced against the control you exercise from the sideline. As with footballers, people are going to be of mixed ability, have different levels of experience and their own personal characteristics. You need a blend of talent to bring out the best effect.

Managers can, if they are not careful, contribute to the de-motivation of staff through their own behaviour. Therefore avoid the following pitfalls:

- Refusal to delegate.
- Being inconsistent.
- Withholding praise.
- Lacking clear vision.
- Not keeping staff informed.
- Being off hand or aggressive.

Similarly, individual team members can affect team cohesion through their own negative behaviour, including:

- Creating their own power base.
- Copping out.
- Harbouring hidden agendas.
- Rubbishing new ideas.

Disgruntled staff can have a very negative effect on staff morale, and then can bring others down with them. To counteract such a situation you must hold on to the clear vision and exact a commitment from staff to follow this common cause. In a group situation, where staff are signed up to a common purpose, the group itself will deal with die-hards and you will be able to sit back as a silent witness to the team's self-cleansing ability.

However, on a cautionary note, when the team is committed to the vision and the mission make sure it is the right one! It is all too common, particularly in large or complex organisations, for professional staff to form cliques and to behave as if the corporate level is nothing to do with them. Worse still, they may depict 'management' as the font of all ills. Therefore, there is a job to be done in linking everything the team does back to the corporate mission and strategic objectives. The team must take responsibility for its corner of the action and understand that others have a different job to do, but all to a common purpose.

To get the best of your team you will need to give them plenty of support. Nurture a team culture where there is an open learning environment. Encourage the proffering of ideas, where things can be discussed and looked at from various perspectives in an open, honest, way without fear of ridicule or reproach. Teams that have a high level of trust among members have better morale and a keener sense of loyalty towards each other. Do not allow personal comments or attacks to be made at team meetings, or rows to break out. If there are problems to resolve focus the team on the problem, never on an individual. Do not accept problems without some proposed solutions. Similarly, if you have taken a course of action that turns out to be wrong, put your hands up. You are a part of the team too, with a responsibility to be accountable and an entitlement to be supported. Good communication is important for effective team functioning, and a ready-made forum for this activity is the team meeting.

Team meetings

Consider in the first instance the purpose of team meetings. In essence they are, like any other meeting, a tool to facilitate decision-making, to exchange information, to generate ideas and to initiate actions (Amos, 2000). As manager you must take responsibility for the running, content and outcome of the team meeting.

Good communication facilitates good teamwork. The team meeting is an ideal opportunity to share information in a constructive manner. Do not confine yourself to internal matters of the team; bring news from the corporate level and from the outside world. It is disempowering for staff to hear about developments on the grapevine rather than from official sources. Encourage staff to contribute information as well as receiving it. It should be a bottom-up top-down process. The team meeting is a forum where teamwork should be evident. They should be behaving as a team, not like passengers on a bus who just happen to be occupying the same space at the same time.

When actions are decided upon ensure that the person or persons charged with delivering the action are clearly identified and that time frames are put in place (Harris and Kelly, 1991). If there is a lot of teasing out to be done on an issue it is not always best done in a big group. You may find it beneficial to establish a sub-group to go away and do a little spade work and report back to a future team meeting. This represents a good use of time and appropriate delegation.

With regard to the running of the meeting it is important that you exercise control. This can be done by actively chairing the meeting and through the agenda. This does not mean that you have to rule the proceedings with an iron fist, but it is important that people stick to the agenda and then limit their comments to what is relevant. As with any group you are going to have people with a lot to say, regardless of the subject and their knowledge of it. Such people usually have a hard neck; so do not be afraid to be very directive with them. If they are a persistent problem work out a battle plan before the meeting, and enlist allies to help you fight your corner.

Encourage all participants to contribute to the agenda. If you consistently find that you are the only one contributing, this suggests that the meeting is not having the relevance for the team that it should. In such circumstances re-visit the purpose of the meeting and make sure you have the balance right between decision-making, information sharing and initiating actions.

Encourage quiet people to participate. Do this more by creating a favourable environment where a timid person may have some hope of getting a word in edge-ways. Never nail a participant; they should be encouraged to speak rather than forced to do so (Amos, 2000).

Watch out for rivalries and alliances. Cliques can be formed in many ways and for many reasons. This in itself is not necessarily harmful. Once basic ground rules, such as respect and tolerance, are in place you should be able to manage. However, team meetings should not be allowed to be a forum to divide and conquer: it should be more a case of one for all and all for one.

As a means of conflict resolution look for compromises. Do not waste valuable time with circular argument. If an issue has been around the houses a few times and cannot be agreed upon, it is a good idea to set up a working group. Appoint an equal amount of people with opposing views and tell them to bring the matter back to the team meeting when they have agreed a way forward.

Finally, make team meetings compulsory. They are an important part of the fabric of the team and a good means of gluing the team together. If you allow an individual to opt out, they are indicating to fellow team members, in effect, that they have something more important to be doing with their time. Obviously, if someone has a legitimate reason they may be excused. Therefore, at the top of the meeting, list any apologies and the reason for them. If team meetings are working right, people will look forward to them. Get into the habit of starting and finishing the meetings bang on time; people will soon realise that you mean business. After the meeting leave some time to have a bite to eat or a coffee with anyone who can hang around; it is a simple, yet effective, bonding opportunity.

Supervision

The concept of supervision is an intrinsic part of practice in the social care professions. In essence its purpose is threefold, to hold the supervisee accountable, to contribute to their professional development and to provide support (Clarke, 1996). This latter purpose of support is the trademark that distinguishes it from other forms of accountability and learning. I remember once a nurse manager, whose office was next to mine, asked why I spent so must time supervising people since they were all trained professionals. It was an innocuous enough remark, but it set me thinking. At the time I was a single-handed manager with seventeen staff, so it was very time consuming. I concluded that the element of in-built personal support for staff was a distinguishing feature of social care, which differentiated it from the more hierarchical professions such as nursing or medicine. That is not to say that the other professions are less stressful but in social care it is the nature of the beast to explore, to express feelings and to debrief on the job. We are just not in a 'do as I say' profession.

The process of professional training provides a professional socialisation whereby the worker enjoys considerable operational autonomy that is free of external direction. However, supervision does provide a form of internal direction or professional guidance. By its nature much of what is undertaken in social care are non-uniform tasks in uncertain and unpredictable contexts towards the achievement of diffuse and often ambiguous objectives. As such these conditions argue for the desirability of supervision (Kadushin, 1992).

In overall terms the key supervisory functions have been described as (Bunker and Wijnberg, 1988):

1. Articulating and continuously adapting the unit's service model.
2. Monitoring individual worker development.
3. Fostering individual worker development.
4. Developing teamwork capabilities.
5. Participation in agency planning.
6. Representing the unit and its performance to other parts of the system.
7. Co-ordinating work activity.
8. Clarifying goals and tasks within the case.
9. Promoting problem solving.
10. Managing the unit's daily operations.

More and more supervisors are held accountable for the professional practice and effective functioning of their team. Therefore it is important to have a system in place to monitor what is going on, and supervision fits the bill. It provides a structured opportunity to talk about the work, review progress and plan ahead. Through this process any difficulties the supervisee is experiencing can be ironed out and targets can be set. Simultaneously the supervisors need to exercise authority, as the process allows them to influence and control the supervisee. This ensures that appropriate things are being done, and in an appropriate manner. In terms of clinical practice supervision is an effective way in which a more experienced practitioner can impart knowledge. However, from a pure management perspective there are a few things that one needs to get right.

The management of supervision should start with a policy. For a kick off you might want to start with a statement that your team, or organisation, is committed to the practice of supervision. Among other things, this can act as an attraction to potential staff that are window-shopping. Similarly it may help to ward off potential supervisors who do not favour structured supervision and prefer to take things on the hop. The policy should ensure equity by making sure all staff have equal access to a similar process. If you are managing supervisors who will be undertaking the supervision, you need to be sure that they are all taking a standardised approach. Therefore the policy should cover issues such as frequency and duration, content, confidentiality, agenda setting, records, conflict resolution and evaluation and review.

The frequency and duration of supervision will vary depending on the experience of the worker. A probationer should expect more supervision than an experienced hand. It may well be, depending on your particular clinical setting, that the task of supervising is delegated to senior practitioners. If you do have front line managers under you supervising staff, you should consider this as a delegated function. As such you need to keep an eye on things, albeit from a distance, because even though someone else is fulfilling the supervision task it is still your responsibility to ensure that it is effective and standardised across all supervisors and staff. In effect, you are supervising the supervisors. In any event, collective wisdom suggests that supervision should be held at least monthly and for not more than one hour's duration.

The content of supervision should commence with a review of the current workload. Consider any actions that were decided upon at the last session. Discussion of the workload will also reveal any skills or knowledge deficit in the interviewee which, after all, is one of the functions of supervision. This may well have implications for training and development. As manager, it is worthwhile having a look at the aggregate needs of staff in this area, for there are obvious benefits in providing collective solutions. However, the needs of the individual cannot be lost sight of and needs to be met, one way or the other.

Effective supervision should be built on a good foundation of respect and trust. This may take time. I once had a poster on my office wall which read, 'I'll pretend to trust you if you pretend to trust me'. Almost by definition the relationship is not an equal one because it is implicit that the supervisor possesses superior knowledge. Confidentiality must be present, but it can only be conditional. Matters may arise where it is appropriate for the supervisor to inform the line manager. The supervisee may wish to flag a personal matter that is having an effect on their performance. Again, confidentiality must be present and any disclosure on information to others outside of supervision should only be on a strictly need-to-know basis. Always remember, there is no place for counselling in a supervision session, so make sure this ground rule is established (Northern Area Health Board, 2004)

Prepare the agenda in advance, bearing in mind that it a two-way process. There should be no surprises in supervision; it is more productive when both parties enter it with their eyes open. Start by following up from the last session.

It is appropriate to keep a record of each supervision session, so that decisions made or action points can be re-visited. It does not have to be a tome; the main points, decisions and actions will suffice. Ensure that any case management decisions are recorded on the case file. The supervision record is ultimately the property of the employing organisation. Therefore, your policy needs to incorporate any data protection or freedom of information safeguards and obligations that may prevail in legislation or other employer policy.

Where a difference of opinion or conflict emerges both the supervisee and the supervisor should make every effort to resolve matters between each other in the first instance. After all, you are in the problem solving business! Failing that, the line manager is the most obvious choice for mediator. However, it may be considered appropriate in certain circumstances, to bring in an outsider as independent mediator. Either way, these means of mediation stand outside any disciplinary or grievance procedures and must be seen as such by all concerned.

Build in a little evaluation and review into the supervision process, just to check on how things are going. This allows some quality time for both parties to review objectives and to tweak the focus if necessary. Do this at least annually and preferably twice a year. It is also no harm to review your policy from time to time. The ebb and flow of staff contributes to the experience and the learning of the team on a continuous basis and it is appropriate to occasionally reflect on this. Exit interviews are a good means of assessing the quality and relevance of both the policy and the practice of supervision: people are at their frankest when they are leaving. Another way is to conduct a satisfaction survey among existing staff. A confidential survey is best for facilitating brutal honesty.

The supervision contract should be an agreement between the supervisor and supervisee on their respective roles. This may require some negotiation and, as such, might appropriately be dealt with in the first session. Agree all the ground rules in the first couple of sessions as well as the broad objectives and any particular issues.

Some organisations allow for external supervision, where the supervisee avails of outside expertise. Typically this might occur, for example, in a small non-profit organisation where the board of management are all lay volunteers. As a general rule however, it is best that supervision is provided in-house as it is a core function in most social service settings.

If you are a single-handed manager you will need to see everyone, so schedule this and ring-fence it. There is nothing more frustrating and demoralising for a supervisee than to be told the boss had to cancel the supervision appointment to do, by implication, something more important.

Appraisal

Appraisal is akin to supervision, but with less emphasis on personal support and with a sharper focus on measurable performance. Given the central position of supervision in the social services, appraisal might be seen as an unnecessary overlap. However, it can have particular benefit if you are managing supervisory staff. It is a good means of judging performance against an explicit yardstick.

In the normal course of events you will be discussing cases and run of the mill issues with your supervisors. However, once or twice a year it would be worthwhile to set aside some time for an appraisal interview. Set measurable goals and standards and then judge performance against them. Consider how your supervisors are doing in relation to corporate and local objectives. Assign tasks, clarify roles and functions and make any necessary changes.

Since most of the time you will be discussing the performance of others with your supervisors this provides you with an opportunity to discuss their own performance. Give constructive and systematic feedback. Be straight, and avoid personalising any difficulties. Hammer the problem, not the person.

Build in a system that ensures supervisors have a standardised approach to managing their set of workers and review this in the appraisal interview. The appraisal interview is, of course, a two-way street, and as such it affords the supervisor an opportunity to express any concerns and to address any training needs.

Delegation

Delegation is the very best way of making the most of your time and that of your team. Not only will it free you up to do the important things that only you can do, but it will also get the most out of your staff. Effective delegation empowers your staff, leaving them feeling trusted, useful, and (if you pitch it just right) challenged. Conversely, failure to do so will leave them unskilled and demoralised. So, newly appointed managers beware: manage what they can do, and do not do what they can manage.

As well as being an example of good time management, delegation is an effective means of staff development. It is good to stretch people. Beginners may need a little TLC but more experienced staff can be trusted with greater responsibility. In fact, it is a good means of assessing the strengths and weaknesses of individuals. Achievers will be identified for succession purposes and the training and development needs of weaker staff will be identified. You will benefit too because it will sharpen your leadership skills.

Start by delegating routine jobs and minor tasks; you need to free yourself up for other, more important, tasks (Roebuck, 1998). If others can do it as well, or better, let them at it. They may require a little lead in time to get the hang of it, but this is an investment well worth making. It may well be that individuals will have some areas of expertise that are superior to yours. Do not be threatened by this but use it as a resource to benefit the team as a whole. Being a manager does not mean you have to be the best practitioner.

When you have decided what to delegate pay attention to how you delegate. Make sure your instructions are clear and unambiguous. Furthermore, ensure that they are understood. It is also important that any required time frames are stipulated explicitly. When a task is delegated monitor progress: remember, you are still in charge. The cardinal rule of delegation is hands off, eyes on.

When the task is completed evaluate the process in conjunction with the member of staff. Give feedback, and make sure it is factually correct and specific. The purpose of the feedback should be to assist, never to undermine. If praise is due be generous; it will cost you nothing. It is a miserable trait in a boss to take without thanks.

Delegation does not have to be confined to an individual, but can be equally applied to a group of individuals. You may wish to delegate a task to your team, or to a sub-group of it. Similarly, delegation can be directed laterally, that is to say, to a peer. It is useful to build bridges with peers of equal rank and function. As well as providing a valuable source of mutual support it also provides an opportunity to share work or to join forces as appropriate.

Lastly there is delegation upwards. It is vital to find a way of working with your boss that will support a sustained relationship. It does not have to be a love-in but the basic elements of mutual respect and trust must be present. Communication is important. Find out what your boss expects and try, where at all possible, to anticipate their needs. Be loyal: do for your boss what you want your staff to do for you.

Managing under-performance

As has been stated in Chapter 2 people perform better when they know what is expected of them. Therefore, develop performance requirements for all staff that report to you. Fundamentally, staff need to know the reasons why their job exists and what you consider to be the most important aspects of it. Every job exists to achieve some organisational objective. By establishing key result areas each subordinate is clear about what is required of them (Hannaway and Hunt, 1995).

The ability of a staff member to meet expectations depends not only on the level of competence and motivation of the individual but also on the level of leadership and support they receive from managers. Therefore, resist any urge you might have to floor someone as a first line of attack. Consider instead any factors for which you have responsibility that may be contributing to the problem. The following questions will help you clarify matters (Hannaway and Hunt, 1995):

- Have they enough support and guidance?
- Is the job too demanding or not demanding enough?
- Do they fully understand what is expected of them?
- Do they have sufficient resources (time, money, and staff)?
- Have they the ability to do the job?
- Do they have the necessary skills and knowledge?
- Are there reasonable explanations for poor performance (family, medical problem)?
- How do they compare to colleagues doing a similar job?

Having considered these questions, and if you have clear evidence of a performance discrepancy, you may then approach the individual. However, do not go down the road of equating the individual as the problem, but rather see them as an individual with a problem. After all it is the behaviour you are trying to alter as opposed to the individual.

In as much as you can, put them at their ease. If at all possible take a joint approach to identifying and agreeing upon the reason for the discrepancy. Here you can rely on your professional skills of listening and assessing the problem. Listening requires considerable concentration so be sure to pick a time when you are not going to be distracted by other matters. Give the person all the time they need to state their case. Decide and agree upon whatever remedial action is required. If there are resource implications, those are your side of the bargain so make sure you can deliver them. Agree a time scale and monitoring arrangements, and always set a review date before the end of the meeting (Armstrong and Baron, 2004). Explain the likely consequences if the required standard is not met within the agreed time frame. Be supportive in manner and tone but firm in your resolve.

By way of a summary checklist Armstrong (1999) provides a seven-step approach to managing performance:

1. Identify areas of under performance.
2. Establish the causes.
3. Adopt a problem solving approach.
4. Ensure the necessary support.
5. Monitor progress.
6. Provide additional guidance.
7. As a last resort invoke disciplinary procedure, starting with an informal warning.

At a policy level every organisation should ensure that performance requirements and standards are explicitly defined, performance is monitored and staff are given sufficient feedback, training and support to meet the required standards. Likewise, the risk of under-performance can be reduced when adequate support systems are in place, when impossible demands are not made of people and when work allocated is within the person's capability to carry it out (Armstrong and Baron, 2005).

'Problem' people

It has been said (Honey, 1992) that there is no such thing as problem people, only problem behaviours. As with under-performance, it is the behaviour that needs to be tackled rather than the person. Even the nastiest, most heinous individuals are likely to have some redeeming attributes, so it is best not to brand them as 'the problem'. However, we all know that some people can be difficult to engage or manage. Nor is it confined to subordinates: bosses who change the rules all the time can be a real handful, as can peers who are unreliable or truculent.

Honey (1992) has identified fifty everyday people problems. Listed below is a selection of my personal favourites:

- Buck-passing: it happens in organisations where apportioning blame is the norm.
- Lazy people lack energy and do as little as possible; however, distinguish lethargy due to illness.
- Manipulators engage in dishonest behaviour, manoeuvring people to do something that does not suit them.
- Bureaucratic people believe the answer to everything is to have set procedures and regulations.
- Ditherers are hesitant and indecisive; they are reluctant to make decisions and if they do they become consumed with doubt.
- Martyrs seek attention by leaving you in no doubt that they are doing a good deed at considerable personal expense.
- Quarrelsome people will start a row out of nothing if needs be while the rest of us walk around on tenterhooks.
- Naggers badger and plead relentlessly until they get their way.
- Abdicators believe that once they allocate work it is no longer any of their responsibility.

I should like to add a type of my own to the list; blamers. Blamers behave in the certain knowledge that they personally could do no better even if they tried and that any deficiencies in resources, standards and performance lay firmly at the feet of 'Management'.

In dealing with under-performance it is often the case that the individual either cannot do it (ability) or does not know how to do it (skill). However, behaviour is particularly problematic when it is the case that they would not do it (attitude) (Armstrong, 1999). It will take more than a word in someone's ear to shift a bad attitude. Nevertheless, the same ground rules apply. Meet the individual; identify the problem and the pathways to solutions; monitor and review at a specified date.

People with a bad attitude are usually tenacious and they will rationalise and justify their position until you, at least, are blue in the face. However, be tenacious right back at them. Also, make sure you have all the ducks lined up in terms of supporting evidence before you make your case. As with a client with poor insight, staff with a bad attitude seldom see the problem in their own behaviour and will inevitably deflect it elsewhere. They may need to be shown a yellow card and, if there is no improvement, you may well have to resort to disciplinary procedures.

Grievance and discipline

Employee relations are arguably the most important personnel function, and if the relationship is a harmonious one you will have a contented workforce. The essential methodology is that if there is a dispute you enter into conciliation with the objective of arriving at a resolution. If your agency is unionised respect the role of the staff representative. They are not the enemy and, although they are acting as advocate for the other side, they can play an important part in the problem solving process. Remember too that they will play that part even if the employee is blatantly in the wrong; it's their job. A union representative once said to me 'Paul, if Adolf Hitler was a member I'd defend him to the hilt!'

It is important that there are explicit, written, grievance and disciplinary procedures; this is not something you want to be making up as you go along. Some of the basic ingredients include the necessity to investigate any disciplinary matter or grievance fully, and to allow the employee to respond, before taking any action. It is appropriate to take into account previous performance and track record. Allow the employee to be accompanied by a next friend or representative, if they want to. Unless there is clear evidence of gross misconduct, dismissal is not an option for a first offence.

Before you can dismiss someone the onus is on you to be able to prove that the employee is either incapable or guilty of gross misconduct. In the case of the latter, gross misconduct will often merit summary dismissal. Examples of this might include gross negligence, abuse of a client, violence, breach of confidentiality, or wilful misconduct (Eyre, 1992).

In the case of the former, make sure that the incompetence is not caused by any lack of training, guidance or supervision that you should have provided; otherwise things could seriously backfire on you. Be very sure of your ground before you let someone go; you may well have to defend your actions before a court or tribunal. That said, you may want to take a calculated risk if you have got someone that is making your life a misery. A moderate hit in a labour court may be preferable to a lifetime of grief.

Finally, never succumb to the temptation to give someone a glowing reference as a means of getting rid of them. It is bad Karma and will get you in the end.

Recruitment

There is a golden rule when it comes to recruitment: employees, like puppies, are for life not just for Christmas. Therefore, never take in strays and never let your heart rule your head. There is very little margin for error when it comes to recruiting the right people, so meticulous preparation is a must.

In the first instance you will need to satisfy yourself that there is a need to take someone on. Do not assume, even if someone vacates a post, that you automatically need to fill it. Consider all the options. What are the essential tasks that need to be done? Are they still relevant? Could someone else do them? Is it a full time job, or could the work be spread around or bought in? Can you promote someone by giving them additional responsibilities and corresponding remuneration? It is worth posing these questions every time it appears necessary to take on a new member of staff. At the very least it will provide you with a justification for the filling of a post.

Job description

If you have convinced yourself that you need to recruit someone the next step is to clarify precisely what tasks the new member of staff is to perform. For this you will need to reflect on your organisation's mission and mandate and to consider what this person is going to contribute to them. Remember, you are looking for someone that will sign up to your mission (Gunnigle, Heraty and Morley, 1997), not someone that will come, do the job and go, like a TV repair man. You want a team player and someone that you can fundamentally get along with.

So start with a job title, something that describes the primary purpose of the job. Some titles tend to reflect the opposite of what they mean. For example, 'Director of Homelessness' might be more aptly described as 'Director of Services for Homeless People'. Avoid limp words such as 'co-ordinator'. If their job is to manage put it in the title, such as 'Manager of Adult Mental Health Team'.

Next summarise the main purpose of the job. You are hiring someone because they have a particular expertise or ability to undertake certain functions, so set out the main function in a nutshell. Then itemise all the duties in some detail. A job description should clarify for a worker exactly what is expected of them, the level of responsibility they have and what authority comes with it. A job description that lists meaningful tasks is a valuable tool for the organisation of work as a whole; it also provides a useful benchmark for the evaluation of individual performance.

The job description should also set out the key relationships, such as whom the person reports to and who reports to them if applicable. It should also stipulate other relationships, for example, works in liaison with, works as part of a multi-disciplinary team, and so on.

It is desirable that the job description should include a statement on pay and conditions. Set out the pay scale, incremental arrangements, annual leave entitlements and sick leave arrangements. If pay increases are dependant on performance, say so. In any event, if you are going to use any form of appraisal (and you ought to be) stipulate this and provide what information you can on it.

At the end of the day there should be no surprises for the employee when they take up duty. If the job description is sufficiently detailed and robust it provides the employee with a clear description of roles, responsibilities and rewards, and it provides the employer with a clear expectation of what is expected of the worker.

Person specification

Essentially a person specification is a description of the ideal person (Gunnigle, Heraty and Morley, 1997). It should be expressed in terms of the candidate's knowledge, skills, aptitudes, experience and qualifications. It is a good idea to grade the individual aptitudes in terms of what is essential and what is desirable. Hence, a very basic person specification will look something like this:

Job Title:

Qualifications	Essential	Desirable
Knowledge/skills		
Aptitudes		
Experience		

When it comes to actually choosing one candidate over another a tight person specification will get you so far, but after that you will still have a few judgement calls to make. In addition to picking someone you think you will get on with, consider also the impact they are likely to have on others in the vicinity and their potential to fit in. It is hard for someone who has not already done a particular job to hit all the exact spots, so look out too for their capacity to adjust and mould into the role.

Screening

Recruitment is a two-fold process: you want to attract the most suitable candidates but you also want to detract unsuitable candidates. How you actually recruit will largely depend on the ground rules of your organisation. Some may be free to headhunt or recruit internally while others may have to advertise publicly. Many employer organisations will have policies on this and, or, agreements with trades union or staff representative bodies. If you have the luxury of being free to decide, consider all the options including word of mouth, colleges, recruitment consultants, advertising in the press, journals or Internet. Think in terms of cost effectiveness as well as communication effectiveness. Spreading the word need not cost a fortune.

Benchmark the candidate off the person specification, not other candidates. It would be premature to start comparing candidates in advance of the interview itself, so stick to facts as to how they measure up to what aptitudes you have earmarked as essential and desirable. Their application should give you a reasonable idea of the candidate's level of attainment, their experience, interests and their purported interests and abilities (Gunnigle, Heraty and Morley, 1997). Where these fit the bill, shortlist those candidates for interview.

Selecting

Some organisations like to precede the interview with various assessment techniques, such as psychometric testing and the like. However, in human services it is difficult to beat the face to face encounter of the interview. In many ways, as a social care manager you are undertaking an assessment. You are assessing a potential employee's capacity to undertake certain tasks, their compatibility to fit into your team, and their motivation to want to work for you and your organisation. Remember; your organisation is on show so fly the flag. You want someone who would take pride in working for your agency.

It is best not to interview alone. A second person will bring another set of observations and opinions and will provide a safeguard in case of disputes. Again, most organisations have policies or ground rules for this. Ideally interview boards should be trained, or at least briefed, on the techniques to be adopted at interview. It is important to have a unified approach to each interview so that you are covering the same ground each time. Divide the person specification between the interviewers, with each one taking a number of competencies from the list. Agree a marking system in advance of the interview and be sure to be consistent when awarding points to candidates.

A candidate that is well briefed will yield more at interview. A good job description will help a lot, but make a pack of any other relevant literature, such as your annual report or strategic plan, and mail it to the candidate in advance of the interview. In the old days the identity of the interview board was a closely guarded secret. However, on balance, it is probably a good idea to advise candidates of the identity and title of the interview board in advance. It will help the candidate to prepare better, and avoid any nasty surprises.

Pay attention to detail, such as ensuring that there are adequate reception facilities, always bearing in mind that the candidate might have a disability. Show respect to the candidate by allowing them the privacy they deserve. For example, do not park them in the public glare and allow sufficient time to ensure they can enter and leave without bumping into the next candidate. This is particularly important in the case of internal competitions where candidates are likely to know each other.

They say interviewers make up their minds in the first few minutes of the interview, and seldom change their minds (Cushway, 1994). It is easy to switch off, especially if you are having a long day of interviewing, but it is important that you retain your concentration. By right your short listing should ensure that you only have good candidates. Listen to the interviewee. Too often interviewers are not listening because they are thinking of the next question while the candidate answers the last one. That is why it is important to prepare interviewers by assigning them competencies to base their questions upon. A bad interviewer is as much a liability as a bad candidate.

There is a growing trend, although it is usually in relation to senior positions, where candidates are asked to make a presentation to the interview board before the interview proper commences. This is usually on the topic of how you would approach the job if you got it. Although it is a daunting prospect for candidates it is nevertheless a great way for would-be employees to get their head around the job and really think themselves into the position. It is probably not fair, or the best use of time, to subject a front line worker to this process unless it is a specialist role such as a teaching or training post. If you are applying for a management position it would be worth your while to prepare a presentation (whether or not you have to make one) setting out how you would approach the job in the short term and the longer term. It is a great way of covering all the angles and of anticipating what you are likely to be asked at interview.

References

When you have made your selection seek references from some one who knows the candidate well and can comment on their capability, reliability and potential (Cushway, 1994). It is worth bearing in mind that some people do a great interview but then fall short of the mark on the job. Often it can be a personality trait that was not picked up, or revealed, at interview. People are at their best behaviour at interviews. They may well demonstrate that they have the required competencies while at the same time manage to disguise the fact that they are a handful. That is why it is so important to collect at least one significant reference. Raise your antenna if someone does not give you their current employer as a referee, and always ensure you get such a reference.

Avoid any temptation to start someone before obtaining references, even if you are badly stuck. It is a bad policy that would land you in trouble sooner or later. Similarly, given that social care is such a sensitive area, working as one does with vulnerable people, it is important to run all the necessary checks, such as police checks, professional registration and so on in advance of the candidate starting work.

Induction

Once the successful candidate is in place it will pay dividends to provide them with a period of induction. No matter how talented an employee is, each will still need a period of adjustment in which to settle in. It is a process of socialisation when new members of staff absorb the culture of the organisation. Introduce a 'buddy system' whereby a peer of the new comer will show them the ropes.

Prepare a pack, manual or at least access to all relevant legislation, policy, procedures and guidance. This should also include the mission of the organisation, its principles and its values. This is a good time to provide the new staff member with explicit expectations of what is required of them. Much of this will be set out in the job description, but there will be additional materials, for example, the 'dos and don'ts', issues pertaining to custom and practice, a code of conduct and so on.

Conversely, the rights of the employee should be set out in writing. This should include, terms and conditions, leave entitlements, statutory entitlements to sick pay, maternity pay, arrangements for trade union or staff representation, maximum hours and any overtime arrangements, any benefits such as family friendly policies and practices, social or sports clubs and any other relevant issues.

In addition to a pack it is always helpful to run an induction programme. Here, experienced staff members, representing all the relevant functions, can brief new staff members and answer any questions. In addition, it may be necessary to provide training if, for example, there is a particular function that your service provides which is a little off the beaten track. A one size fits all approach to staff intake is unlikely to work in today's complex range of social care environments. It is worth factoring in the extra time and expense to produce a customised programme because the benefits will surely follow.

Staff training and development

Just as the issues and needs in social care continuously evolve so too must the skills of the social care worker if they are to grow professionally and respond appropriately to those issues and needs. Managers need to be constantly attentive to the training requirements of staff so that they can perform at an optimum level. This may involve the development and implementation of effective training programmes which afford workers an opportunity to develop and practice new skills. It may also involve less onerous initiatives such as facilitating the dissemination of professional literature, conference attendance, workshops or classes.

Commit to knowledge based practice in a learning organisation. As manager you will need to (Statham, 2004):

1. Know how to access the information that underpins good practice, where the knowledge is weak or absent.
2. Relate this directly to the work of the practitioner.
3. Understand how people learn and how to audit the team's knowledge.
4. Enable practitioners to communicate their knowledge to those using the service.
5. Contribute to the learning organisation by structuring front line information as a resource for the development of the organisation's policies, practices, provision and commissioning.

Main messages

- People who are inspired make willing followers.
- Effective teams agree upon their vision and mission and then agree on strategies to implement them.
- The team meeting is a valuable tool for generating cohesion, decisions, information, ideas and actions – make it compulsory.
- Supervision is effective because it holds the supervisee account-able, contributes to their professional development and provides support.
- Delegation means keeping your hands off but your eyes on.
- There is very little margin for error when it comes to recruiting the right people – meticulous planning is a must.
- There are no problem people, only problem behaviours.

Chapter 4

Managing Strategically

For every complex problem there is a simple solution that is wrong.

George Bernard Shaw

Strategic management is all about forecasting the future. It is the art of selecting future courses of action that direct resources to the highest priority or changing needs. It has been defined as a disciplined effort to produce fundamental decisions that shape and guide what an organisation is, what it does and why it does it (Bryson, 1993).

Taking a longer-term view

The essential aim of strategic management is:

- To provide strategic direction.
- Prioritise the use of resources.
- Set standards.
- Deal with any changes as you move forward.

(Koteen, 1997)

I have come across a social service that was so busy putting out bush fires on a daily basis that it never had the time to plan ahead. The consequence, inevitably, was an awful lot more bush fires. Yet life in the fast lane, although stressful, can also be addictive. Macho management was quite fashionable in social care until relatively recently. I was once with a senior manager at the end of another long, panic-stricken, and yet curiously satisfying day. He leaned back in his enormous swivel-chair, with his hands behind his head, and said 'Paul, planning is for sissies!'

In the fullness of time the same organisation went to the opposite extreme and established a planning department, separate from operations. By so doing it made the mistake of divorcing strategic management from the overall management task. Strategic planning cannot stand alone as an end in itself where the plan belongs to the planners, not the service managers. It must be an integral part of the overall management process. The plan must belong to those with operational responsibility for service delivery.

Even a cursory glance at recruitment advertisements will testify to the fact that human services are recognising the need for forward planning by recruiting more and more strategic managers. That is because they realise, that while most members of staff are stuck in the here and now of service provision, someone needs to be looking to the future.

As a first line manager it can be assumed that a lot of the strategic thinking will take place at a corporate level. Indeed national strategies will be handed down as a given, but nevertheless, every level of the organisation deserves a little 'buy in' to the high level strategy. It is appropriate that you examine it for specific relevance to your team. For example, if a new national health strategy is published, you will want to know what the implications are for your particular functional area. If, for instance, the national strategy promotes more user participation you will need to consider what your team is going to do to meet this new requirement. Customise the strategy for your part of the organisation. What areas are relevant for you to promote, what new things will you have to do and what might you need to do differently? Look at your service in the here and now and consider what alternative courses of action to take in the future. One of the most important tasks of a manager is to develop new ideas and put them into effect as part of the organisation's response to the changing needs of users and carers and the demands on the service (Scragg, 2001).

Benefits of strategic planning

Over and above any strategies that might be handed down from on high it is appropriate that you should undertake some strategic thinking for your division or team. As we know, social care workers are preoccupied with the pressures and demands of day to day work. This pressure often creates a point blank view of the world where staff talk of being at the coalface or in the pits. Preoccupied with these mining activities they do not feel they have the time to look up and see a gap of light at the end of the tunnel. Besides, there is no point because the future is too uncertain (Smith, 1994).

However, as manager, you must not fall into the trap of being too busy to get organised; for if we do not plan ahead, the future has an awful habit of falling in on us like the proverbial tonne of coal. I have a motto that I picked up somewhere along the way:

We either plan, or we resign ourselves to be at the mercy of events.

It is common to find resistance from operational staff, and indeed operational managers, to strategic planning. They fail to appreciate its relevance to their daily hands-on work and view it as a very non-macho activity. It is like trying to get real men to eat quiche. However, strategic planning has many benefits for operational staff as well as planners and policy makers.

For one thing it promotes strategic thinking by clarifying the organisation's future direction. It establishes organisational priorities and converts them into actions, identifying who is to do what, and by when (Clarke, 1997). Decision-making will be improved by focusing on critical issues. Identifying and addressing critical issues will improve organisational performance and changing circumstances can be dealt with more effectively. Staff will benefit from the clarification of roles and by having a logical road map to follow. Therefore, the desired outcomes of strategic planning can be summarised as follows:

- Clear understanding of actions to be taken.
- Increased investor satisfaction.
- Increased user satisfaction.
- Value for money.
- Evaluation to benchmark achievement against goals.

Commencing the process

Strategic planning is a communal exercise; it cannot be handed down like tablets of stone; rather it needs to be built up from the ground. Anyone who is going to be affected by the process needs to be involved and that includes users, other stakeholders and staff at all levels. Also include anyone who has the capacity to obstruct the process. Therefore, make sure your boss is on side and that the employee relationship climate is right. It is useful to commence with some fundamental questions:

- Who owns the plan?
- What is it trying to achieve?
- How will the process be managed?
- How will it be divided into constituent parts?
- What are the key strategic issues?
- How might these issues be addressed?
- Is it for the whole organisation or just a part of it?
- How long is it going to be for?
- Is there a realistic chance of getting it implemented?

The process will also require considerable leadership to drive it forward. You must not only champion the cause for your service but also ensure that it is endorsed by the organisation as a whole, where this is applicable.

Just remember that there are times when it is not a good idea to proceed with a strategic plan. The time will not be right if the organisation is in turmoil and the roof is caving in, if there are insufficient resources in terms of money and skills to see the thing through, if the cost outweighs the benefit, or if the political environment is not right (Bryson, 1993).

Writing a strategy

A strategy is a plan of action committing resources to a particular set of objectives. A good strategy will bring together the organisation's major goals, policies and action plans into one forward-looking, cohesive, initiative (Mintzberg and Quinn, 1992). Set objectives that support that strategy in key functional areas. If yours is a big organisation it will already have a strategic plan. So create your own strategy, linked to the corporate one, but make it totally relevant to your aspect of the service. This is your chance to stick your head out of the bunker to take a longer-term view of the future for your team. The main elements of a strategic plan should include:

- Your mandate or raison d'être.
- Mission and vision.
- Guiding principles and values.
- Environmental analysis, including organisational structure and links to the external environment.
- Likely changes or challenges into the future.

- Identification of strategic issues and key priorities.
- Implementation.
- Monitoring and review, including performance indicators.

(Clarke, 1997; Cole, 2003)

If you prepare well, using these ingredients, writing the strategic plan will be a piece of cake.

By now you are familiar with the need to be very focused on your **mandate**, which is the reason why you go to work in the morning. Nevertheless, preparing a strategic plan provides an opportunity to review and clarify your fundamental raison d'être. As has been mentioned elsewhere, a mandate for a social service may be derived from legislation or national policy. Other possible sources include research reports, evaluations, articles of association or the constitution of your particular organisation (Courtney, 2002).

You are now also familiar with the need to have a lofty and inspirational view of how things can be, based on your mission and vision. The **mission** is all-important in social care as it defines what you stand for and reinforces that intention to really make a difference in someone else's life. Review your mission to ensure it is still entirely relevant to today's environment.

Many organisations, particularly in business, drop the **vision** statement settling solely for the mission statement. However, particularly in social care, a statement of vision can provide additional inspiration as to what you are ultimately trying to achieve. So, set out in a sentence what outcome you would want to see if your mission was fully successful.

Allied to this is the concept of guiding **principles** and **values**. These represent your ethos, your philosophy and your culture. Ironically, and particularly in social care, different parts of the organisation may have different cultures (Courtney, 2002). This will most likely be prevalent in large, complex, organisations with a multi-disciplinary component, such as a hospital, or community based teams that have a number of functions or disciplines. It is particular to social care because, as we have seen, the social care worker's primary loyalty is to their profession, not employing organisation. Therefore, if you feel the need to customise your values for your particular division, the following words may have some resonance for you:

- accountability
- equity

- confidentiality
- trust
- integrity
- empathy
- partnership
- client-focused
- needs led
- quality driven

An **environmental analysis** entails, in the first instance, an internal analysis. Take a good look at your current **organisational structures** and how they are best equipped to the challenges ahead. Consider the functions currently assigned to staff and their relevance to meeting the strategic objectives. Review current activities in relation to your staffing, funding, service users and, where relevant, technology and information requirements. This should be done not only in consultation with staff, but with suppliers, customers and other stakeholders. In essence you want to look at how things work as well as what works. Be bold at this phase; if a service component is not working, or is not as relevant as it used to be do not be afraid to re-jig it. Too often complacency sets in where people say, 'but this is the way we've always done it'. However, such an attitude is putting the service before the consumer. Do not lose the opportunity to re-configure services by making them more relevant by directing them in a more focused way on actual need. If social services are not needs led they are not relevant. Therefore, if a service is hopelessly off the mark, abandon it and re-direct the money to where it is needed most.

Analysis of the **external environment** should involve an examination of your services position in relation to key stakeholders such as funding organisations, government organisations, suppliers (those who make the referrals), specialists (those to whom you make referrals), consumers, staff representative groups and the public.

Consider social factors, such as demographic trends. There is little point in a service turning out excellent pre-school placements when the population has grown up and actually requires day care places for older people. Social factors may also include changes in societal values. When I started out 'unmarried mothers' were, almost by definition, a cohort of the community that required special help and were singled out for it whether they sought it or not. Society has moved on, and so too must the services.

Similarly, in parts of Western Europe there has been a huge influx of foreign nationals, mainly from Eastern Europe and Africa. Many of these are asylum seekers with multiple needs and services are on a steep learning curve as they come to terms with new challenges such as language requirements, cultural norms, ethnic diversity as well as meeting considerable health and social needs. Human services run into serious difficulties where they fail to adapt to such changing needs (Courtney, 2002).

Political considerations may also constitute a social factor. A government could introduce a new law or policy that radically affects your day to day work. Therefore, try to predict any such likelihood, remembering that change can bring opportunities as well as risks. In this regard it is helpful to undertake a SWOT analysis.

SWOT stands for:

- Strengths
- Weaknesses
- Opportunities
- Threats

Having undertaken this analysis you will be in a position to identify the **key strategic issues**. This entails the identification of key things your service, as a whole, needs to do to respond to new and emerging need. It is the art of matching needs to deeds. For each issue you identify, an appropriate action needs to be developed. Be economical when it comes to making choices about the future direction of your service; a half a dozen is plenty. It is better to identify a handful of **key priorities** and achieve them in the designated time frame than to reach for the stars only to realise that gravity has pinned you down.

The main reason why you are setting objectives is to set targets against which you can measure performance. Therefore, as with the service plan in Chapter 2, make sure that they are **SMART**:

- Specific
- Measurable
- Achievable
- Realistic
- Time bound

Within your strategic plan the inspirational items, such as mission, vision and values will not change much over time. It is only when you begin to implement your strategic plan that you will really get down to business. As Peter Drucker (1990) puts it, good intentions do not move mountains; bulldozers do. He argues that, in non-profit organisations, the mission and plan are the good intentions and strategies are the bulldozers. Therefore, it is necessary to convert what you want to do into achievable tasks that are readily understood to those charged with performing them and easy to communicate to all concerned. This is where your annual service plan, or business plan, will feed off the longer-term objectives by prioritising tasks on a year by year basis thus chipping away at the overall strategic objectives.

Next, in order to benchmark achievement against objectives it is necessary to put in place a process to **monitor and review** progress. As has been stated earlier this is not an easy task in social services. It is not as simple as indicating a profit margin and one has to rely more on less tangible indicators of success. **Performance indicators** are the tools to use in measuring outcomes, as discussed in Chapter 2. This is recognised as the most difficult aspect of strategic planning within a social service context.

Ideally you would like to be able to demonstrate that someone's life is better because of the intervention of your service. However, in reality you may have to rely on qualitative data such as client satisfaction ratings, rather than more empirical evidence such as client condition. Likewise with quantative information you may have to rely on bread and butter data such as the numbers using the service, waiting times from referral to intervention, and so on. In any event, the trick is to link the PIs to the overall strategic objectives and to gather what information you can that will show you what progress is, or is not, being made towards the achievement of those strategic objectives.

The duration of a strategic plan can vary. Many are five-year plans, yet this seems a little long. Others are three-year plans and this seems a little short, yet I never heard of a four-year plan. As a general rule the more uncertainty there is in your working environment the shorter the duration should be. Social care is continuous and recurring in nature and as such a long term plan may become outdated before it is achieved. So, do not assume things will remain the same and do not plan too far ahead.

The successful **implementation** of your strategic plan will require the guiding hand of a good leader. Strategic objectives need to be built up by staff with the assistance of a leader who promotes excitement about the road ahead. An important element of building up your strategic plan is to involve staff at all levels in all stages of the process. The strategic plan is a great means of providing meaning and purpose to overall team effort. If the plan does not resonate for front line staff who are doing the actual interacting with your client group it is not relevant. Therefore, use this as an opportunity to excite staff with a compelling vision of what the future can hold. It is a very powerful message for them to realise that they can and are making a difference.

Finally, critical success factors include:

- Having crystal clear objectives.
- Consulting widely and deeply.
- Maintaining the initiative.
- Being flexible.
- Monitoring, and amending where appropriate.
- Directing resources where they are needed most.
- Implementation on a rolling year on year basis.

Strategic leadership

Anyone who manages people will inevitably be involved in a modicum of strategic leadership. As team leader you will be keeping an eye on the bigger picture and steering the overall direction of the team as well as managing the bread and butter issues. In essence you must (Gilbert, 2005):

- Set a clear vision for the future.
- Set out the steps to achieve the vision.
- Align the mission to the team in order to achieve specified goals.
- Meet current objectives while building for the future.
- Manage change effectively.
- Inspire and empower members of the team.

You will need to keep in touch with developments at national level and be aware of the prevailing political environment. Acquaint yourself with all relevant legislation and policy and connect your service to them. Audit what policies are in place for your service and if there are deficiencies make sure that you fill the gaps.

Familiarise yourself with other departments and know how their functions connect with yours. Identify the key stakeholders and develop a nose for the dynamics of the organisation as a whole. You will be expected to contribute to the overall strategic planning for the organisation. In this regard you need to link your team to the mission of the overall organisation, keeping your people motivated and motoring.

Gather information from a variety of sources in order to inform your decision-making. You may well have standard statistical returns to make. In addition you have at your fingertips a wealth of information concerning referrals, service users, service requests, waiting lists, care plans, reviews and so on. Convert this data into management information by analysing it and picking out the salient messages. Numbers are neutral things that have to be interpreted, so consider what the information means for the delivery of your service. It is amazing in social care how often activity data is collected for statistical purposes at organisational level, but never actually used at team level because everyone is too busy running around chasing their tail. So, start at the other end and use your head by putting information to work in the form of messages for practice.

Closely associated with information is communication. Decisions are made based on the information available and these decisions need to be communicated effectively in a variety of directions. Develop a clear communications strategy so that you will know who needs to know what, without having to make it up each time. Ensure that the rationale behind your decisions is comprehendible and readily conveyable. Remember that you may well need to communicate upwards as well as below, or latterly into other functions or externally to the outside world.

Indeed, as a strategic leader you are the interface between your team and the external environment. That external environment is wider than the immediate stakeholders, but also encompasses the wider social milieu. A good way to examine the wider external environment is to apply the PEST exercise, political, economic, social, and technological (Osborne, 1996; Smith, 1994). Fill in the boxes as they relate to your service, for example:

Political	Ecomonic
Change of government	Economy
Legislation	Staffing costs
etc.	etc.

Social	Technological
Changes in societal values	New technology
Demographic change	Communications
etc.	etc.

Outsourcing

As a busy front line manager there will be things that you will not get around to that you really want to, or ought to. In such circumstances it is worth considering farming this work out to an outside source rather than leave the work undone. Outsourcing can come in a variety of sources, such as research, evaluation, consultation, professional or academic expertise, or the full scale sub-contracting of a service area or function.

The commissioning of **research** is a valuable tool if you want to generate some empirical evidence into a particular area of interest. You may wish, for example, to profile a cohort of foster carers in order to better understand their motivation to foster, with the further aim of refining your recruitment techniques. Form associations with research and academic institutions so that you can keep in touch with emerging trends and best practice. Social care workers are not good at this compared to the medical and nursing professions and there is often a hiatus between what is being taught and what is being practiced.

Evaluation is a useful way of determining the benefit of a particular service. The benefit can be measured in terms of outcomes for the client or value for money, or both. It is particularly useful when establishing a new service to build in an evaluation element that will take a reading after, say, the first year. It is easier to tweak things while they are still at a formative stage. **Consultation** can be a useful way of taking soundings. For example, you may not want to undertake a full evaluation of a service but you might benefit from an expert second opinion in relation to a particular aspect of a service. Likewise, **professional or academic advice** might add value to a service by contributing to best practice. You may wish, for instance, to have an expert sit on an advisory committee that reviews issues in relation to the provision of a new or specialist service, such as a residential unit for sexually aggressive adolescents with a learning difficulty.

However, do not 'dumb down' your team by assuming the expertise does not lie within it. Normally outsourcing would only apply when the team is too busy to provide the necessary reflective time, or when the expertise actually is not there. As a general rule the involvement of hands-on staff adds benefit to any examination of a service or issue. It also facilitates 'buy in' in relation to the final conclusions, especially if charges have to be made that affect front line staff.

Tendering

If you are investing money in an outside source to undertake a piece of work on your behalf, it is vitally important that you nail down the issues you want covered. Therefore clarity of purpose is the key. There are a number of headings that will help in this regard:

1. Introduction – describe, in a few paragraphs, the background to the service and how it came about that you want some outside help.
2. Services provided – describe all the service elements that are to be examined.
3. State the purpose of the desired assistance required, for example:
   - To examine the range, nature and quality of services provided.
   - To analyse and evaluate the effectiveness, relevance and appropriateness of the service.
   - To examine funding arrangements in terms of cost effectiveness and value for money.
4. Methodology – this might include literature review, practice review, interviews, consultation with users.
5. Stipulate the budget limit and required time frames.

Committing your requirements to paper will be as helpful to you as it will be to the person tendering, as the exercise demands clarity. As a rule of thumb, if you cannot write down what you want in a few sentences, the chances are it cannot be done.

Service agreements

The sub-contracting or commissioning of a service is in a different league to a once off project, such as an evaluation. For example, a statutory service may wish to commission a voluntary organisation to provide a particular service because of its perceived expertise, flexibility or capacity. In such circumstances the service is, in effect, being delegated outside the primary service. Bearing in mind that the principle of delegation is hands off, eyes on, adequate monitoring systems should be put in place. In addition, ground rules in relation to funding levels and levels of services to be provided should be clearly spelled out. In short, you need a service level agreement, which in essence is a contract between you, the commissioner, and the service provider.

A service agreement can take many forms, but ought to contain some fundamental and non-negotiable elements:

- Target group – a description of the people you want the service provided for, including the need to be met and age range where appropriate.
- Aims and objectives of the service to be provided.
- Catchment area – state any relevant geographic boundary to the service.
- Funding arrangements including the total amount, payment arrangements, timescales and a schedule of costs.
- The quantum of service to be provided, i.e. the number of placements, the number of clients at any one time.
- Staffing – an itemised breakdown of staff by grade and salary.
- Description of referral procedures.
- Monitoring – state the arrangements that will be put in place to review, monitor, evaluate and inspect as appropriate.
- Any other local requirements, such as insurance, health and safety, complaint mechanisms, adherence to relevant policies and procedures.

Once you have the fundamentals in place you can afford to do the flowery bit on partnership, shared mission and values. Also, ensure that the agreement is signed by an appropriate person form both parties. It is also useful that the document should name a key person form both organisations to act as a conduit into each service: this facilitates communication and avoids confusion.

Main messages

- We either plan or we resign ourselves to be at the mercy of events.

- Strategic management is the art of selecting future courses of action that direct recourses to the highest priority or changing needs.

- A strategy is a plan of action committing recourses to a particular set of objectives.

- Set objectives that support the strategy in key functional areas.

- Measure how you did, not what you did.

- A strategy is a plan of action committing recourses to a particular set of objectives.

- Set objectives that support the strategy in key functional areas.

- Good intentions don't move mountains – bulldozers do.

Chapter 5

Managing for Quality

Quality is doing it right when no one is looking.

Henry Ford

The 'customer' in social care

A porter in a centre for homeless people once said to me: 'I can't keep this place tidy with all those lay-abouts lounging around'. This provides a graphic example of how to completely miss the point regarding the purpose of one's job. He was putting the condition of the building before the condition of the person that the building, and he, was there to serve.

A quality service, therefore, is one that meets the customer's requirements (Oakland and Morris, 1998). In the business world the motivation to produce a quality service is competition. To make a profit a business must produce a product that satisfies, or indeed delights, its customers. The same motivation is not present in social care. Consequently, in human services, the concept of quality and that of 'customer' is generally not as well developed or clear-cut.

The vast majority of customers, or clients as we refer to them in social care, voluntarily seek a social service as they might any other service or product. However, reflecting on the discussion on eligibility criteria in Chapter 2, they may not always get what they want, in the quantity they want or when they want it. Therefore access is a big issue for social care customers. A social service that is flooded with referrals is always at risk of succumbing to the temptation to pull up the drawbridge, leaving a mote between the client and the service provider. Public criticism will often assert that obstacles are being put in people's way. Whereas commerce seeks to expand the customer base as far as possible, because customers equal profit, social services tend to go heavy on the gate keeping as a means of controlling intake.

In addition to access there are issues such as consistency, standards and flexibility. People want to be treated as individuals rather than having to fit into a service criterion. Too often social services start by listing off the types or people and cases they do not take; in other words they take a service-led approach. A quality social service, on the other hand, will start by determining the needs of the client, thus taking a needs-led approach.

A problem facing human service managers generally is the lack of 'fit' between the client's needs and the services they actually receive. This can, in fact, be compounded in services where there is a multi-disciplinary element. Each discipline has its own area of expertise and responsibility. Since clients often require the assistance of more than one discipline there is always the potential for rivalry, overlap and the occasional bruised ego (Christian and Hannah, 1983). This is a scenario that requires careful and sensitive management.

It is not so long ago that the commercial world relied on the 'hard sell' whereby products were simply pushed onto customers. More recently this has been largely superseded by the concept of 'customer care'. In this model the needs of the customer come first. Information on products is more honestly presented in the belief that such trust will be rewarded by the loyalty of a truly satisfied customer. Satisfied customers come back to people they trust. Likewise, in social care, trust is all important. It is a fundamental characteristic of the relationship between the helping profes-sional and the client. However, a distinction needs to be made here between trust and dependence. In social care the goal is always self-reliance; you want the client to trust you but not to become dependent upon you.

Customer care often goes beyond the point of sale to provide an after sales service as a means of ensuring ongoing customer satisfaction. The social care equivalent to after sales service is 'follow up' or aftercare. The psychiatric hospital will follow up the patient through home visits or out patient appointments. Social services will provide an after care service to the young person leaving care. Therefore, this concept of customer care can be easily imported into social care practice for, ironically, it is based on the principle of helping people to help themselves.

The involuntary client

We all make grudge purchases from time to time, such as paying out money to the dentist, insurance companies or lawyers. We do not want those services but we know we need them (Cartwright, 2000). It can be argued that many social services are the grudge purchases of society. For example, no one likes paying for new prisons but they are very convenient when we need somewhere to put the bad guys.

When I worked in the area of child protection there had been occasions when I had the duty to forcibly enter people's homes, armed with a warrant and a group of police officers, to remove the children from the household. In such circumstances it would have been disingenuous, to put it mildly, to subsequently ask the parents what they thought of the service.

Social care is often faced with this dual responsibility to society's most vulnerable members on the one hand and to society as a whole on the other. In fact this dual concept of change agent versus social control agent is expressed in the American National Association of Social Workers code of ethics as follows:

> *Social workers treat each person in a caring and respectful fashion, mindful of individual differences and cultural and ethnic diversity. Social workers promote clients' socially responsible self-determination. Social workers seek to enhance clients' capacity and opportunity to change and to address their own needs. Social workers are cognizant of their dual responsibility to clients and to the broader society. They seek to resolve conflicts between clients' interests and the broader society's interests in a socially responsible manner consistent with the values, ethical principles, and ethical standards of the profession.*
>
> (NASW Code of Ethics, 1999)

Continuing with the child protection analogy, it is not immediately obvious who the customer is in such circumstances. Is it the children who require care and protection, even though they did not seek it, or is it society that demands that they are kept safe? I remember struggling with this concept at a management development course years ago, only to realise I was sitting between two prison wardens. If I had a dilemma they must have had a catastrophic predicament!

Yet, although a prisoner has no choice but to be an inmate, they are still entitled to a good quality service. Hence, it is evident that a unique feature in the public sector is the concept of the involuntary client. Perhaps the most recognisable form of the involuntary client is the psychiatric patient who has been committed 'for his or her own good'. In effect, they are treated by psychologists, psychiatrists and nursing staff as 'pre-voluntary' clients (Rooney, 1992). In such circumstances the service may not be wanted but it is required. As such the quality agenda can apply to involuntary services because they seek to meet the customer's requirements, even though the customer did not personally determine those requirements.

Rooney (1992) distinguishes three different types of 'reluctant' clients:

1. Involuntary – those forced to seek, or feel pressure to accept, contact with a helping professional.
2. Mandated – those who must work with a practitioner because of a legal mandate or court order.
3. Non-voluntary – those who have contact with a helping professional through pressure from agencies, referral sources, other persons, family members or outside events.

Traditionally social care is associated with the voluntary contract but clearly there are mainstream service professionals, such as prison workers, mental health workers and child protection workers that balance a dual mandate between the individual client and society as a whole. Again, Rooney (1992) poses a number of questions that such practitioners want answers to:

- Who is the client?
- What do I owe the person before me, the agency and society?
- Can I use authority legally, ethically and effectively?
- When do I intervene against a person's will and when do I not?
- Is the only alternative coercing the client with a requirement or ignoring problems when there is no requirement?
- Can I remain sane and avoid burnout?

Of course, one choice of action open to the helping professional is to ignore the fact that the client did not seek the service and to proceed as if they did.

The features of quality management

A good reputation is hard got, easily lost and very difficult to win back. Just think of your last bad meal out. Therefore, reliability and consistency are key features of quality management. Quality cannot be bolted on at the end of an intervention; it has to be built in from the start. The process is all-important. Process is everything we do to create a service. Like baking a cake there are raw materials (ingredients) and there are methods (recipes). By getting everything right at this input stage we are guaranteed a quality output, or product (Oakland and Morris, 1998). It is a piece of cake really. This simple act of due diligence from the beginning shifts the emphasis from inspection at the end to prevention from the start. Therefore, quality management is about preventing problems from arising in the first place. For this to be achieved there must be a clear understanding of the customer's requirements. Each member of staff involved in a process should be very clear about their respective roles to satisfy this requirement.

Unlike other areas of management, quality management cannot be delegated from those at the apex of the organisation. Neither can senior management impose it. There must be buy-in at all levels from the top down. A degree of leadership is required whereby everyone is facilitated to take responsibility for their area of work. It requires the development of a culture that commits to continuous improvement and the principle of prevention (Brocka and Brocka, 1992).

In essence, the mission of the organisation needs to be broken down into a series of processes that will address the achievement of that mission. For this to happen critical success factors should be identified that are directly linked to the mission. They should be measurable and might include areas such as timeliness, cost effectiveness, performance and so on.

Everyone in the organisation must be aware of what they have to do in their particular area to bring about the achievement of the organisational mission. To do this effectively at every level requires positive working relationships, or teamwork. Once all levels are bound together in a common cause the organisation becomes one single entity with the common objective of putting the customer on a pedestal. The re-orientation process to create a truly client-focused service requires an investment in staff. In the first instance they deserve respect, and recognition that they are the organisation's most valuable resource. As the re-orientation requires a fresh look at how things are done, and how each individual might improve their own work processes, staff need appropriate training and support.

Good ideas do not communicate themselves; they need to be conveyed through good communication processes (Oakland and Morris, 1998). It is an essential requirement that every level of the organisation is informed of the change process and that all staff are signed up for it and prepared to take ownership of their area of expertise. This pre-supposes that staff accept the need for improvement and embrace the concept of main-streaming quality management into their everyday work practices. It will take continuous communication, in all directions, to maintain the unity of the organisation as a single entity going forward.

When all these features are present and operating smoothly it is referred to as **Total Quality Management**. Total means that everyone in the organisation is involved. Quality means that the service is meeting the required need. Management means that quality is achieved through a process, not by co-incidence. Its essential elements may be summarised as follows:

- The customer must be satisfied.
- The organisational goal is total quality every time.
- There is commitment from every level of the organisation.
- Quality must be measurable.
- Improvement must be continuous.

Applying quality to social care

Although the profit driven motivation of the business world is not applicable to social care the core elements of customer care are (Bee and Bee, 2001):

- appropriateness
- consistency and reliability
- timeliness
- customer satisfaction

By delivering on these core elements at the client level a social care organisation can become a quality service. In terms of **appropriateness** people want a service that sees them as individual and unique. They want services to be flexible and customised to meet their particular needs. As such these services will take into account people's lifestyle and culture. Appropriateness is therefore linked to what is known about best practice and to agreed professional standards. Appropriate social care must be both clinically effective and suited to the needs they address.

People want services to be consistent. Public expectation is thwarted when services vary from place to place. For instance, if the home help can visit a dependant adult three times a week in one catchment area but only once in another, dissatisfaction and complaints will follow. Therefore, to be **consistent**, services must comply with minimum standards. Often national standards apply to specific areas of social care that regulate how services are operated. In addition some professions have their own code of conduct, which help to provide consistency and quality in service delivery. In many jurisdictions, too, Social Service Inspectorates have been established. These inspectorates certainly contribute to driving up standards and improving accountability. However, inspection in itself is not a quality assurance measure in that it is applied 'after the fact', that is to say at the end of a process. Quality cannot be added on at the end; like a car coming off the assembly line, quality must be present from the design stage to the finished article (Oakland and Morris, 1998). On the other hand, the continuous monitoring of services does provide quality assurance in that it ensures standards are up to scratch in advance of any inspection taking place. It is too late to lock the stable door after the horse has bolted.

Timeliness can relate to the accessibility of a service as well as the responsiveness of a service. Waiting lists and boundaries are obstacles to services. It is a simple fact that an unmet need is likely to exacerbate over time, thus requiring more social service time and money in the long run. Therefore, early intervention can promote effectiveness in terms of service delivery and cost.

Fair access is a prerequisite to a quality service. It relates to making the same quality of services available to people in accordance with their needs, regardless of their location, social status, gender, age or cultural ethnicity. Ensuring that services are responsive is a management function. Good leadership is required to ensure that services are delivered in accordance with best practice, which is derived more from internal review rather than external inspection.

A social service, whether imposed or sought, should always aim to provide the service user with as good an experience as possible. A child in care may not want to be there but they will want the best possible experience. Satisfaction will also be generated when services are provided that build on people's abilities rather than their vulnerability, and when they are included and provided with choices. This is referred to as a strengths-based approach to service provision.

Removing barriers to quality

At organisational level barriers can block quality service provision. A classic symptom of this is when departments work within their own function with no connectivity to those working in other departments. Each department works in an independent silo serving their own objectives. Typically in such circumstances the following management style is present:

- Decisions are taken at the top with little insight into their implications.
- Front line staff are not consulted.
- Little recognition of the staff who are working face to care with the user.
- Staff are working for the boss rather than the end user.
- Trouble-shooting is substituted for longer term solutions.
- Decisions made at the top are not communicated effectively.

The knock-on effect for employees is that:

- People work as individuals rather than as a team.
- Back room staff feel no connection to the customer.
- Staff feel excluded and left in the dark.
- Management is not trusted or respected.
- Staff feel under valued and disempowered
- Staff turnover is high.

(MacDonald, 2003)

These are all symptoms of a traditional bureaucratic organisation where senior management dictates, operational management controls and workers do what they are told. One way of getting out of the silo mentality is to employ one of the features of Total Quality Management, namely the process chain. A **process chain** exists when each service element is linked to the next across departmental boundaries with the ultimate aim of satisfying the customer. The chain is as strong as its weakest link so the trick is to ensure that the links are of equal strength (MacDonald, 2003). This also involves a shift in management style. Old-fashioned top-down bureaucracy is replaced by a more flexible approach where continuous improvement is everybody's objective, staff are listened to and included. Decisions, with supporting rationale, are communicated well at every level of the organisation. In such a customer-focused environment the following features will be present (MacDonald, 2003):

- Innovation is encouraged.
- Staff input and feedback is actively sought.
- Staff are supported in meeting the needs of the customer.
- Decisions are explained and communicated widely.
- Long-term solutions replace quick-fix solutions.
- Collaborative goals are set to promote teamwork.

Performance management as a quality initiative

Performance management is a way of ensuring quality by promoting high standards in terms of efficiency and effectiveness, equity and value for money. It is also a means of holding people accountable at all levels of an organisation. This is done by setting goals and by establishing measures to assess progress (as detailed in Chapter 2). This is particularly important where social care organisations may have a monopoly position. For example, in many jurisdictions, if a couple wish to adopt a child, they will not have a choice of agency and must seek to be assessed by the local state child care agency. Since profit and competition do not apply, there needs to be another form of motivation to promote quality and this can be done by imposing **standards**. Standards are a set of values, principles and criteria that ensure a uniformity of service delivery at a consistent level.

Clear **accountability** arrangements should be put in place at every level of the organisation. Procedures need to be established for dealing with poor performance and bad practice. The primary reason for this is to protect vulnerable service users. Managers are responsible for quality control on their team, but to be really effective there needs to be corporate support for the concept. This will be particularly relevant when the poor performance of an individual is being challenged. If the person being fingered fights back, for example through union representation, the line manager will need the support of the corporate organisation.

The acid test for managing performance is to spend a little time asking the obvious question, is this service working? Strangely enough, there is no real history or culture in social care of measuring **outcomes**. People tend to get stuck into problem solving without a clear idea of what exactly they are trying to achieve. This relates back to clarity of purpose, as discussed in Chapter 2. The essential task of social care is to improve the well-being of the individual. Therefore, whatever the intervention, it should be possible to put a marker down as to what the desired outcome might be.

For example, parents attending a parenting skills programme should have identifiable new skills at the end of the process. However, it is not always as simple as 'curing' someone. Sometimes the objective may be to maintain the quality of someone's life rather than to change any particular aspect of it. For example, a service may be concerned with maintaining a person with a learning disability in the community. It is clearly impossible to remove the disability but it is possible to improve their quality of life by, for example, improving their life skills and enhancing their personal environment.

Other useful questions to ask are, could we do it any better and could we do it differently? Consideration of doing it better is a quality initiative that challenges compliancy and seeks to improve effectiveness. Consideration of doing it differently introduces dynamism and opportunities for improving efficiencies.

Very often, perhaps too often, customer satisfaction is relied upon as the sole measure of success. Clearly the user view is important, and should be factored into any outcome assessment, but it does have its limitations. For example, if a homeless person attending a day centre says 'I think you people are wonderful', it does not tell us anything about whether or not their needs are being met or their welfare has been improved as a result of their attendance. Therefore, it is worth factoring in consideration of **client condition** as well as satisfaction. Is the individual better off for having used your service?

Another highly relevant question would be, is the service worth the money? We all have a keen sense of **value for money** when it comes to personal purchases. The greater the sum of money involved the more we deliberate. For instance, you would not impulse buy a car like you would a bar of chocolate at a checkout. It is far more likely that such a purchase will be preceded by considerable research and agonising. We ought to bring these same good habits to the workplace.

As manager you are responsible for the stewardship of resources under your control. Even if you do not have direct responsibility for a budget you still have resources in the form of people and services. These resources must be deployed and allocated in a manner that will optimise the benefit to the user. Time is money; therefore how it is spent equates to financial expenditure. Ensure that you are making the best use of staff time.

Keep in mind that services that are not working to optimum effect can be re-jigged or decommissioned altogether and the money put to better use. So, be creative. There is an increasing emphasis on managers being made responsible for the choices they make when designing or delivering services. Performance is often viewed in terms of costs as well as quality. Delivering services to an agreed or set standard is a good way of achieving efficiencies in terms of quality and cost. Funding agents will want to know what added value your service is providing, in other words are they getting sufficient bang for their buck. It pays to have a well worked out answer that can demonstrate the effectiveness of your intervention.

The same issues arise if you are commissioning services; you will want to know what you are getting for the money (see Service Level Agreements in Chapter 4), and whether that service is bringing an added value that you cannot provide as effectively or efficiently through your own service.

Linking knowledge to practice

As alluded to earlier, there is a need to link emerging thinking and learning to current practice. Too often social care operates a twin-track between college-based learning and community-based practice, and never the twain shall meet. This contrasts sharply with other professionals, most notably the medical profession. It has an in-built mechanism to promote continuous learning, through journals, seminars, tutoring and so on.

Experience alone is not enough to perfect practice: it must be combined with ongoing learning. Therefore, attention should be paid to sources of learning in an ongoing journey of discovering how things might be improved and done better. A number of immediately evident sources exist, such as your own observations, the views of your staff, messages from research, external stakeholders such as inspection agencies, the press and public opinion and feedback from service users (MacDonald, 2003).

At a fundamental level you must have a good grasp of national, regional and local legislation and policy that impacts on your service; this should include the local administrative and regulatory requirements. This in itself will assist in assuring that basic standards are maintained. Take nothing for granted, however, and ensure that you regularly monitor that the service is indeed adhering to these fundamental requirements. Complacency and inattention are the hallmarks of poor management.

A feature of a quality service is the active participation of staff in contributing to improvement through a process of constructive feedback. The views of operational staff should be actively sought. Staff on the ground have a keen sense of what works and what does not, and they will also have a well developed sense of what works elsewhere. So, you might want to give some thought as to how to harness this information in a systematic way.

Closely related to this is the requirement to keep staff up to date with emerging practice and research findings. It is useful to form associations with services elsewhere, including other jurisdictions. It is remarkable how often the wheel gets re-invented for the want of sharing knowledge. Good ideas can be bartered with other services, although usually you will find that you are pushing an open door and services are flattered to be asked to impart their 'superior' knowledge.

Likewise, there is great benefit in linking with learning institutions to see what emerging research can contribute to good practice. Academic findings contribute to an evidence based approach to practice, rather than relying on a finger in the wind or an attitude that advocates that this is the way we always do it. To overcome being stuck in a rut or overwhelmed by complacency, innovation and big ideas should be actively encouraged.

This may require a culture shift for not all organisations value ongoing learning. Neither can the blame always be laid at the feet of senior management. It is often the case, particularly on teams with a high-pressure function, that running in the fast lane is rewarded and reflection is frowned upon as useless navel-gazing. Those with the 'fire-fighting' roles are respected most with others being perceived as having a cushy number. In such a macho environment there is little opportunity to stop to consider what works best or what might be done differently. However, we know that a quality service must strive for continuous improvement and this can only be achieved by reflecting on current practice. As manager you need to make two things happen. Firstly, the busyness must be punctuated occasionally where your 'fire-fighters' are forced to take time out and to have a considered look at what they are doing. Providing the odd day away from the office to reflect upon performance might have the desired effect. Secondly, an ethos must prevail whereby the mantle of champion does not rest with the warrior alone. Remember, in a quality service the process chain links each service element to the next and none is more important that the other. The old adage holds true that for the want of a nail a battle can be lost.

It is a management function to ensure that staff training and development is sufficiently robust to deal with emerging trends and needs, otherwise practice will lose its cutting edge. As well as creating a culture that values second line activity as much as front line activity, there must also be recognition that ongoing training and development is everybody's responsibility if excellence is the ultimate goal. The macho mind-set that equates a day's training to a day wasted needs to be re-directed so that ongoing training and development is seen as an essential element in the creation of a quality service.

External forces can influence the raising of standards. Where formal inspections exist they do have the effect of promoting improvements. Although, as discussed earlier, they are not a quality measure in the true sense as they are applied at the end, rather than from the start of a process. Standards that are set should be based on available evidence and best practice. They will be improved and maintained by ongoing monitoring. Public opinion can also influence practice and, if the issue is big enough, public representatives and the media will also get in on the act. For example, if minors are persistently being admitted to adult psychiatric services because there are no more appropriate facilities available, this might easily spark considerable public interest via the local media. Emotive issues can bring huge downward pressure to bear on services, often seeking to influence service priorities. That is one reason why clear eligibility criteria (see Chapter 2) are important. In that way you can demonstrate that you are providing services in as fair a way as possible within available resources.

The ultimate test of a quality service is how the users perceive it. Therefore, the view of the service user should be collected in a systematic way so that it might inform practice and influence change where it is needed.

User participation

It is invariably the case that the nearer a social care worker is to the client the less they get paid. This investment of status in the hierarchy says as much about the position of the client as it does about the front line worker. It also follows that if power is invested at the top the workers interfacing with the client are disempowered. If they have little power delegated to them, it means, at least to some extent, that their ability to say 'yes' on behalf of the client is restricted. This all goes to show that where services do not put the customer first other needs are being met besides those of the client. In such a situation it is not uncommon to pick up an attitude that suggests the service is great; it is just the clients that are bad.

Such a scenario is indicative of a service that is provider led rather than needs led. When power and authority are held at the top the customer can only be a benign receiver, an observer rather than a participant. To be a real participant the user must have a stake in the decision-making. They must be able to affect the outcomes; in other words, they must be presented with choices.

Most services are designed for 'standardised' persons. In such a one size fits all approach the assumption is made that all people need the same thing. Decisions about service delivery are usually pre-determined before the user is even engaged. This is all very well if one is turning out garden gnomes, but in the people business clients, more than anything else, have a fundamental desire to be treated as individuals. As Oscar Wilde put it, 'consistency is the last refuge of the unimaginative'.

We have seen that a feature of quality management is the minimisation of variation in the process. However in applying this concept to social care it relates more appropriately to processes, such as assessment frameworks or eligibility criteria, than it does to the service user. Quality social care will distinguish itself by being able to customise the service to meet the specific needs of the individual. A consistent finding from client surveys is that users feel that they have to adapt to the way the system works rather than the other way around.

In order to meet individual needs the social care worker has to be prepared to do a lot of listening in the first instance. Service users may have different interests to service providers, so there has to be an initial process of negotiation. You would not walk into a tailor or a hairdresser without stating your requirements, or at least your ideas. As part of the service you expect to exchange views before agreement is reached on a way forward. Likewise in social care one should consult before decisions are made rather than operate on the basis of foregone conclusions. Effective consultation requires meaningful dialogue.

Remember too that professionals have a habit of speaking a language that the stranger does not know. As George Bernard Shaw put it: 'all professions are conspiracies against the laity'. Users cannot participate if they do not know what is being said, so there is no place for jargon if there is to be an honest exchange between provider and user. There is no need to set oneself up as an 'expert'; the needs of the user will be more effectively met if authority and governance are shared. Clients do not want to be entirely passive or compliant; they want to form a relationship with the service based on mutual respect.

Advocacy

Social care workers are well used to the broad concept of advocacy as a core value. They advocate meeting the needs of individuals by speaking up on their behalf; they advocate for groups that share a common need and they advocate for entire constituencies, such as the disabled, the disadvantaged or the poor. Social care workers are also familiar with service users organising into groups, such as self-help groups that advocate their own needs, interests and concerns.

Social care can also be a vehicle for advocacy in the area of policy reform. Promoting values such as social justice, fairness and self-determination are fundamental to social care. So too is the promotion of the well-being of clients, consumers and citizens by influencing the shaping of human service systems (Bruce, 1999).

However, advocacy can go a step further. It is all very well when you are advocating on behalf of someone in relation to another service, but what about where a client takes on an advocate to assist them to influence decisions that affect the services that you provide? Suddenly the tables are turned and the social care worker may feel threatened by someone encroaching on their comfort zone. There is an inclination to get on one's high horse and say, well; after all I have done for them! Yet, there is no point in getting defensive; if advocacy is good enough for other services it is good for your service too. It is in effect an additional quality assurance where the client is facilitated by an independent third person to navigate a smooth course through the service. It need not be seen as a black mark against the service; indeed the openness of a service to embrace it might well be considered a quality initiative.

We are, perhaps, most familiar with the concept of legal advocacy where someone, perhaps a minor or a dependant adult, will have their interests independently protected by someone such as a *guardian ad litum*. Outside of the judicial system advocacy can be provided on a more informal basis, such as, a client wishing to bring a friend to an interview with social services as a means of moral support. There is an opportunity here for your service to build a quality feature into its policy by actively encouraging clients to nominate a next friend to act as advocate in their dealings with your service.

Ensure that your service has a mechanism in place to support vulnerable people in the journey through your service. Such a mechanism must take into account the need to develop the confidence and the knowledge of the users so that they will be more inclined to speak up for themselves. In addition it is good practice to liase with the advocate or other representative groups to facilitate the user to provide constructive feedback, or to complain where necessary.

Complaints and appeals

Most people will know how infuriating it is when having made what is considered to be a well-founded complaint, reasonably stated, to be given the cold shoulder. It is a sure way of adding insult to injury. Even if there is a level playing pitch vulnerable people are not going to feel comfortable about making a complaint. They often lack confidence and feel, indeed often are, disempowered. Therefore, in order to balance things up, a little positive discrimination is required.

Clients who feel that services have fallen short of the mark must be facilitated by having easy access to a complaints' mechanism. A prerequisite to this is that it should be well publicised and inviting in nature. Ideally complaints should be received by a named individual who is free to act as an independent third party to review both sides of the argument. Complaints should be received in a positive manner without any hint of defensiveness; after all it is feedback that might help to improve your service. Active consideration should be given as to how vulnerable people can be enabled to voice dissatisfaction. Again, an advocate may facilitate this, perhaps from a representative organisation. Clients are already likely to feel at a disadvantage because they are complaining about the system to the system. Therefore, every effort should be made to assure them that their complaint will be taken seriously and reviewed independently.

All the same principles apply to appeals. Where a user is dissatisfied with a decision they ought to have the right to have that decision reviewed by someone else. As with the complaints system it should be well published, easy to access, with the assurance that people will always be treated with courtesy and respect.

As responsiveness is important a good complaints or appeals system will have standard time frames. Sometimes complaints are difficult to unravel and a resolution may take some time. In such circumstances it is important that the reviewer keep in touch with the complainant to apprise them of developments.

Remember that staff have rights too. In the first instance all staff should be well informed of the complaints and appeals procedures. Due regard should be given to their side of the story. The process should be as blame-free as possible, concentrating instead on systems rather than individuals. It is the problem that should be tackled rather than any individual member of staff. Consideration should also be given to the training requirements of the staff who handle the complaints, covering the basics of customer care, empathy, conflict resolution and plain English.

The receipt and processing of complaints is an opportunity to promote quality in the service. A legitimate complaint that is satisfactorily resolved may well have broader implications of the service as a whole. Lessons can be learned that can have the effect of raising standards and improving the overall service.

Where complaints cannot be resolved locally there should be a mechanism to refer the matter to a higher authority within the organisation. Of course, any internal complaints mechanism does not diminish the client's right to petition external authorities, such as an Ombudsman or any other authority that might be relevant to a particular jurisdiction.

Clients' charter

A nice way of demonstrating commitment to customer service and quality is to set out that commitment in the form of a clients' charter. Such a charter is a public promise to set and maintain standards that are people-centred and rooted in best practice. As with the introduction of a quality system in general, a clients' charter should not be imposed from the top: it needs to be developed from the bottom up, involving staff at all levels. Typically a clients' charter would cover the following areas:

- quality
- accessibility
- information
- timeliness
- complaints and appeals
- participation
- choice
- staff

In the first instance get staff to agree upon a statement that sums up the nature of your service and the **quality** that users may expect. Then frame it and hang it on the wall in the reception area. I once visited a hostel for homeless teenagers in New York City and it displayed a framed mission statement in every room; it was very inspiring.

Prepare a simple, no frills, description of what your service does. Resist all temptation to start listing what you do not do. How often have you seen service descriptions that start with, we do not deal with persons over 65 years, people with learning disabilities, addiction and so on? By all means set out your eligibility criteria, because the more explicit you can be about what you do the better.

Accessibility is of fundamental importance in social care, starting with physical access. It is hugely embarrassing, and fundamentally unacceptable, to have physical barriers to a social service. Ensure that your building is accessible to wheelchair users and that there is a wheelchair accessible bathroom. This will cover you for all eventualities, such as parents with young children in push chairs, older people, people with sensory disabilities, and the like.

Accessibility should also cover issues such as opening hours, geography and equity. Your service should be open at a time that suits your clients, and that may not be nine to five. Where people live should not be an obstacle to receiving a service so consideration will need to be given to issues such as distance, outreach services, and satellite clinics as appropriate.

Next consider your reception area. It should be clean, tidy and welcoming. Your reception is the gateway to your service so you want to make a good impression. This includes your receptionist, whether on the phone or at a desk in the front hall. The people fronting your service should ideally be trained, or at least coached, in the niceties of meeting and greeting. I once brought a Danish colleague to a centre for homeless people. As the door was locked I rang the bell (with a pencil as it was covered with an unidentified sticky substance). There was a barred window to the side of the door. It opened: a porter's head pressed against the bars as he offered a gruff, yes, what? My Danish colleague turned to me and asked: is this how you greet the public? So, remember Chapter 1; you do not get a second chance to make a good first impression.

Consider too the possibilities that information technology brings nowadays. Websites, computer generated forms, e-mail and **information** that can be downloaded can be a godsend to busy people or to those who are house-bound. It is also available on a 24/7 basis, so it opens up all sorts of possibilities for you to be doing business even when you are tucked up in bed.

Timeliness is a big issue for any customer. A fundamental deliverable is that services are provided with courtesy and respect. Introduce a policy that phone calls are returned and that mail is responded to within a prescribed time frame. The fundamental act of communicating with people helps to placate them. If you do not have all the answers at least tell people what you know: it is their information you are holding. Do not avoid people; it is so rude.

Describe your **complaints and appeals** system in simple and inviting terms. The client charter is also an opportunity to invite feedback, good or bad, on how people perceive your service. You might be surprised at how people on the receiving end can come up with sensible and practical suggestions for improvement.

More formal feedback will be gleaned through a systematic consultation process with staff. **Participation** means that you devise ways of facilitating people in setting out the real issues that affect them. These views should feed into the planning process, as services are being developed and delivered. In order to ensure that the views expressed are as representative as possible it is useful, where possible, to have formal consultation with representative groups that have a stake in the services you provide.

People like to be given the flexibility of **choice**. This can range from opening times and location to language. Make sure any written material is sensitive to ethnic minorities, and customise it to suit people where you can. There will be times when you cannot say 'yes' to people, prevented perhaps by legislation, regulation or policy. In such circumstances you should at least be able to demonstrate fairness and empathy.

There are two aspects to including **staff** in your clients' charter. In the first instance they are agents of your service. As such they will require some collective training in order to ensure a consistent approach to the public. When staff are being inducted they need to learn the seriousness with which your service commits to quality and customer service, so commit to this in the charter. Secondly, staff may be viewed as internal customers with needs of their own. Ensure that you have mechanisms in place to support staff and to consult them on every step of the way. If your staff are unionised approach this in the spirit of partnership and set out this open approach in the charter.

Main messages

- A quality service is one that meets the client's requirements.
- The quality agenda applies equally to involuntary clients.
- A good reputation is hard got, easily lost and difficult to win back.
- Good ideas do not communicate themselves: they need to be conveyed through good communication processes.
- The core elements of customer care are appropriateness, consistency and reliability, timeliness and customer satisfaction.
- Continuous improvement is everybody's business.
- Develop meaningful ways of involving users.
- The ultimate test of a quality service is how the users perceive it.

Chapter 6

Managing Change

Imagine . . .

Inscription at the Strawberry Fields Memorial, New York City

The times they are a changing

One thing is certain in this world; change is here to stay. Life itself is dashing along at a ferocious pace and it has no reverse gear. Take the technological advances, for example. When I was small my father would take my sister and I out into the back garden at night to watch the satellites going overhead, like shooting stars that blinked. The world was still full of awe for Sputnik, first launched by the Soviet Union in 1957. No bigger than a basketball, it sailed across the heavens orbiting Earth in just over an hour and a half. Later, as a teenager, I watched the Eagle as it landed on the Moon, live on TV. Then, in a fit of teenage pique, I grew impatient with how long it was taking Armstrong to take his one small step so I went to bed before he did. A few years ago I visited NASA with my family. Discarded spacecraft were lying around like garden furniture. One had a sign beside it that read 'photo opportunity'.

When I first started as a social worker in the late seventies I luxuriated in the fact that we were issued with free biros and notepads. Years later, when we acquired our first fax machine a member of staff wanted to know what part of it one spoke into! Now we dispatch e-mails to the four corners of the earth at the touch of a button. We are all working in an ever-changing environment. The pace of change is accelerating all the time as is the rate at which obsolescence occurs. None of us will be working in the exact same way in another few years.

Change: what and why?

In terms of business processes, change is doing things differently than they were done before (Davidson, 2001). In addition to technological change, discussed above, changes also occur in how staff does the business in response to the changing needs and demands of the customer (Great Britain, 2003; Harvard, 1998). In business the customer is a good barometer for flagging a need for change. As we have seen in Chapter 5 anticipating and satisfying customer demand is a necessary skill for survival and advancement in any business or service.

A fundamental reason for change is a belief that things can be done better. In business the drivers for change, in addition to new technology, are likely to be new competition, new market opportunities, financial performance and customer preference (Great Britain, 2003). In social care, however, the emphasis is more likely to be on client need and the best way to meet it.

Needs do change in social care, and services must therefore adapt to remain relevant. Consider, for example, how AIDS has affected the delivery of health and social services in the last couple of decades. I remember, in the early 1980s, coming across someone for the first time that was HIV positive, as a result of intravenous drug use. We did not have a clue of what was to become a new epidemic wiping out street-loads of young people, just as if they had gone to war like previous generations and never came back. Now, of course, there is a virtual health and social service industry dealing with HIV and AIDS.

Changing needs in social care is the equivalent of new markets in the commercial world. For example, you will not be surprised to learn that a charitable organisation known as the Shipwrecked Fishermen and Mariners Royal Benevolent Society went out of business some time ago. Just as the commercial world adapts to emerging trends, so must social services if they are to remain relevant.

Changes in society, demography and the political landscape all have the potential to bring change. So too does the economy. A rising economic tide might bring opportunity in the form of new service developments; a lowering tide might bring the threat of service reduction or downsizing (Heller, 1998a). Therefore, change can be either a threat or an opportunity, but it is best to put a brave face on it by taking a proactive approach.

Change can come from within or without. An example of externally initiated change might be a government decision to re-organise the national health and social services. This has happened in Ireland between 2000 and 2005. Actually, it happened twice between 2000 and 2005, just to be sure! Also, following a couple of decades where there was an absolute dearth of national policy in social care, there followed a virtual avalanche of legislation, regulation, policy, standards and guidance. Likewise in Britain it has been estimated that over 100 volumes of guidance were issued between 1990 and 1995.

An example of an internal change might be a decision to re-organise the service. It might involve downsizing, outsourcing, or an alteration in processes or the way things are done. Either way, change starts when someone, inevitably someone in authority, starts to look at things and gets to thinking that they could be done to better effect if they were done differently. Something happens that activates a need to change in order to meet a new challenge, and things will never be the same again.

Types of change

Change can be incremental or it can be radical. Incremental change is a gradual process over a prolonged period. Aging is an example of incremental change; you do not wake up old one morning, you grow old over a period of time. In social care incremental change might involve the phased implementation of new legislation or a strategic plan. It might also involve changes in work practices. For example, a community-based social work team with a central referral system might decide to devolve from one big team into one intake team and one long term team. This could be phased in over a period of time as old cases are closed and new cases are taken on. The change is typically evolutionary.

Radical change is more like the 'big bang'; it is revolutionary, rapid and dramatic. It could, for instance, involve a total re-organisation of a service from a particular start date. It is typified by sudden and fundamental change. Radical change could also be born out of a crisis, where a major response has to be made to avert or deal with a catastrophe. The 'millennium bug' was an example of the widespread anticipation of a possible catastrophe (Heller, 1998). Hands up anyone who was in a plane at the stroke of midnight!

Change can also be imposed or it can be developed in a participative way. An example of imposed change could be, as cited earlier, a government decision to re-organise health and social services. It might also be a dictate from senior management. This is more likely to occur in large, complex organisations with a hierarchical structure and culture. Participative change, on the other hand, tends to occur lower down in an organisation where staff is given a say in the design and implementation of the change.

Resistance

You can take it for granted that the old order will not go quietly (Davidson, 2001). As a rule people do not like change; they like things the way they are. Change is perceived as something that is done to one (Gilbert, 2005). Fear of the unknown is a big factor in the resistance of change. People get comfortable in familiar surroundings and do not want to risk change by stepping out of the comfort zone. Therefore, change is often perceived as a threat, even if it is not.

Staff will often express a feeling of being out of control. This heightens anxiety and promotes a sense of helplessness. Ultimately it can lead to denial (Evard and Gipple, 2001). There is a cultural dimension as to why people resist change, and it does not necessarily have any tangible foundation. Staff can have an illogical attachment to the status quo (Davidson, 2001). Therefore there can be a large element of emotional resistance, as well as a mental or physical resistance. The solution lies in addressing the resistance at that emotional level. Try to understand the reasons for it and work with it rather than against it. Resist the temptation to reach for a sledgehammer when you meet opposition and consider arming yourself instead with a carrot and a stick. Change, like a new pair of slippers, needs to be broken in gently.

The flip side of resistance is commitment. Getting there requires an ability to understand the reasons for people's unwillingness to move. Examine the issues from the standpoint of the opponent and respect where they are coming from, even if is not the most logical of places. It is the social care equivalent of starting where people are at. Look for common ground; it reduces uncertainty and offers a pathway to agreement. Self-interest is a strong motivation for accepting change. If people can see that there is a benefit in it for them, such as money, career opportunities, an easier way of doing things, they will be much more inclined to shift.

Social care professionals are also likely to commit if a change can be demonstrated to represent an improved outcome for clients, even if it means more work for them. For example, the introduction of a new care plan template for children in care might mean staff having to collect more information than before. However, if it is seen to be worth it in terms of benefit to the client and improved practice standards, staff will usually sign up to it without too much acrimony.

A word of warning; there is often a caucus or a rump in an organisation, particularly a large one, that is totally resistant to everything. Like super bugs, they will not lay down. They have only one view of the world, their view of it. They are the employee equivalent of the Flat Earth Society. Do not waste too much time cajoling them; it is too late, they are beyond redemption. In such cases do not think sledgehammer, think nuclear! Such people need to be given clear and unambiguous instructions, after which you will need to monitor for compliance.

Usually, change will start with a big idea from someone on high. They will be far more concerned with logistical requirements than they will with the impact it will have on the staff group and on individuals. Senior managers often overlook or miscalculate the impact of change on people. They may see it as collateral damage. However, wounded staff do not perform well and tend to hide in the long grass of old, familiar ways. At a human level, change can hurt people. The rug can be pulled from under them, with no one bothering to ask if they are alright. Therefore, it is worth paying close attention to the human consequences of change.

The personal impact of change

One thing that is not going to change is that your staff are living, breathing human beings with feelings, hopes and dreams. They want and need respect and recognition for what they do. They want to feel that they are making a valuable contribution to the service as a whole, and they want to be challenged in a way that will bring about a sense of personal and professional growth (Evard and Gipple, 2001). Most of all they want to be told that they will still have a meaningful role when the change process is completed.

Uncertainty dampens the spirit and de-motivates staff. Disgruntled staff are less productive; so long periods of not knowing are bad for business. Uncertainty is worse than bad news because it prolongs the agony (Hardy, 1996). It is advisable to keep everyone informed as best you can, with as much realistic information as possible (Hardy, 1996). A little bit of handholding is also prudent; your team needs to be minded in times of transition. Telling people to get over it is just old-fashioned macho management. Have a heart; after all this is a caring profession.

Facing major change at work is not unlike the loss and change that is experienced in bereavement, although, obviously, it will seldom be felt as acutely. Most people that have trained in social care will have come across Bowlby's attachment theory where he describes the experiences of bereaved persons (Bowlby, 1969). Change is seen as a loss, and even non-death loss and change can bring grief. Indeed, the traditional thinking in bereavement counselling is that the absence of grief in the face of major loss is pathological (Firth, Luff and Oliviere, 2005).

The loss of major relationships is a cause of bereavement. This can apply in the workplace as well as elsewhere. For instance, the reorganisation of a service may unwittingly smash closely bonded teams, scattering individuals to the four corners, leaving them feeling quite bereft. The abrupt loss of relationships, combined with the other change factors, can leave a person in a state of disequilibrium. It might even be rated as a life-changing event. Modern bereavement theory teaches us to focus on the needs of the individual (Firth, Luff and Oliviere, 2005). Take a leaf from this book and consider the individual needs of your staff members in the face of major change. Bereavement counselling combines practical help with support. You too can provide support by being empathetic and by providing what help, advice and encouragement you can to each individual member of your staff. Support promotes resilience. Resilience is a concept derived from physics and relates to the ability to re-form after a major stress such as bending or stretching. Your staff too will bounce back if they are looked after properly. Do unto others as you would have others do unto you.

Leading the change

This is your chance to ride a white horse and become a champion for change. The change process needs to be led from the front (Great Britain, 2003). Remember, the meek shall inherit the earth only if that is okay with everyone else; so be assertive and take charge of the situation.

Start by creating a vision for people (Broome, 1998). Paint a picture of a brighter future for everyone. Spell out the benefits to be had by the change. Do not just tell them; inspire them (Hussey, 2000). Social care training teaches the social care professional to become an agent of change for the client. In managing change you, in the exact same way, are a change agent for your team. As the change agent, identify where the problems are and consider what opportunities there are for change. Create an atmosphere for change by promoting readiness and a willingness to take a risk.

Uncertainty breeds mistrust so put them in the picture as much as you can. Express confidence in your team and in how they can contribute to the change process. A key objective of a leader is to motivate people. Without motivated people the change process goes nowhere. People are much more likely to sign up for a change if they are involved in making it happen. Imposed change is much more difficult to implement. It is a real irritant for staff to have a change handed down from on high in the absence of any consultation. Therefore, if there is any scope at all for doing so, involve the team at the design stage. Where imposed change is unavoidable your task will be to develop a sense of ownership in the team by encouraging everyone to sign up to it by imagining a better future.

Try to instil a sense of belonging among your team, linking them to the corporate values of the organisation as a whole (Galpin, 1996). Where an individual has a sense of belonging it minimises the 'us and them' effect and greatly increases the likelihood of them embracing the change. If the opportunity exists, go for some 'quick wins'. If you can demonstrate early on that the change is having a positive effect, either on the staff directly or on performance outcomes, your staff will be more accepting.

The timing of change is important. When the reason for the change has been delivered and understood and the vision of a desired outcome has been articulated it is time to inject a little urgency into the proceedings. Briskness defeats inertia and keeps things moving. However there is a balance to be struck. Go too fast and you will start to lose people who will get nervous all over again. Therefore, avoid white-knuckle rides and think more in terms of a brisk jaunt.

Either way, there is going to be a transition period to be managed. Before something new begins something old has to end, and the interim period can be a fairly messy business (Davidson, 2001). It may be that temporary management structures must be put in place. Roles and functions may also have to change during the transition period. This can be a confusing, not to say chaotic, time. Be particularly sensitive to any individuals whose roles are in transition as there can be a lot of ambiguity in the change process at this stage. People are on red alert for any perceived threat to themselves and it will take the poise of a ballerina to avoid treading on toes.

The longer a transitional period goes on the more it breeds uncertainty and weariness. Rumour takes over in the absence of hard facts and the most illogical scenarios can be circulated as absolute truth. This in turn feeds a vicious circle of suspicion and mistrust that can only be off set by concrete information and continuous reassurance. Change needs to be effected, not just talked about.

It can often be the case that there is uncertainty about who is making the decisions about what during a transition period. In such a scenario the work rate drops, as do many heads as their motivation flags. It is in no one's interest to drag out the transition period so play your part in keeping the whole thing as brisk as possible.

There is one exception to the general rule of supporting, informing and involving others during a change process and that is where there is a pending disaster (Hussey, 2000). Ever notice how, normally gushingly friendly cabin crew, become very assertive if there is a safety alert? Their voice is raised; their tone goes mean as they issue short, brisk, instructions. There is no time to lose when the iceberg beckons. In such situations instruct, direct, order, and discipline anyone who is non-compliant (Hussey 2000).

Implementing the change

There needs to be a convincing business case for making a change, because if it ain't broke don't fix it. The change might be strategic in nature; or it might relate to organisational or management structure; it might involve processes or the way people do things. The starting point, therefore, for making a change is to provide a compelling argument for doing so (Galpin, 1996). As part of this process it is appropriate to ask some fundamental questions, such as 'What is the purpose of our service?' and 'what particular benefits do we bring?' This links back to your mission, as discussed in Chapter 2 and brings clarity of purpose for what you are doing and why you might want to do it differently.

Describe what the situation looks like right now. Then project it to what you want it to look like after the change. It is also a good idea to pick a halfway mark and to set an actual, and realistic, date for getting there. Develop very clear objectives, which will serve as your road map on the journey. Personalise things for people, telling them as precisely as possible what it is going to mean for them (Evard and Gipple, 2001). People are entitled to know what their individual roles and responsibilities will be. A good plan of action will also be flexible so that it can react to an unforeseen obstacle or an unplanned change.

Most changes will work best through a phased implementation. It is important to set goals because they focus everyone's mind on the task. In the case of a corporate change that will affect your team or division, set goals for your staff that are linked to the strategic level. In this way the actions of your team will be relevant to the strategic direction and staff will easily see that they have a part to play in the overall corporate change. They will also feel like they have been involved in the change process. It may be appropriate to prioritise some key areas for change in order to take a bite-sized approach to implementation. A realistic time frame will also help.

How you communicate the change process is a vital success factor. Communication is more than just imparting information; it is also about hanging around until you hear the penny drop. Social care professionals know a thing or two about presenting information, often upsetting information, to people. So, sensitivity is an issue. As a social care worker would do with a client, the message needs to be repeated a number of times and in a number of ways. Staff will need space to digest the news and come back for further exploration and dialogue. Communication should be viewed as a two-way street. Your staff will require opportunities to question and to provide feedback as well as receive information (Galpin, 1996).

Be honest and tell it the way it is in an empathic manner. Get in there before the grapevine; otherwise you will have to spend a lot time debunking myths before you get on to the actual reality. This way you will strengthen relationships rather than antagonise people, and it will promote confidence in the leadership. If you do not know the answers do not spoof. Go and find out if you can and, if you have to, say you do not know. Too many 'don't knows', however, look bad and are a strong indication that either the change process has not been properly worked out, or there is actually no need for it in the first place. If a straight question has you tied up in knots you are probably on to a loser. In such circumstances adopt the Homer Simpson philosophy: if at first you don't succeed, forget it!

An assessment of your staff's training and development needs is essential. At the very least change cannot occur without an exchange of knowledge. This will be done through your communication process. However, upskilling may also be required to adapt staff to the new situation. I remember once, as a social work manager, making a case for training to a senior manager only to be told, 'Sure, didn't you all go to college?' If only it were that simple; but training requirements are themselves subject to continuous change. Knowledge itself becomes outdated and constantly requires to be refreshed. Factoring in training and development needs ensures that human needs are captured as well as logistical requirements.

Another element that is required is a change of attitude. An attitude may be founded on knowledge, but it may equally be based on ignorance. That is why a learning process must take place. Attitude is also closely associated with motivation. You need people to behave in a different way in order to effect the desired change. This comes back to appropriate leadership skills; making things happen rather than making people do things. The development of a culture that supports a learning environment will help greatly in this regard.

If the change is big enough and complex, such as a complete organisational change senior management may establish a Change Team. A typical change team will comprise a variety of employees in order to obtain a skills mix and a comprehensive knowledge of the business as a whole. It is best to take staff from each level of the organisation in order to get a range of perspectives as well as the skills mix. Some of the more hierarchical organisations tend to go with the philosophy that staff, like children, should be seen and not heard. Such a philosophy is 'old hat'; any implementation plan will be enriched by the contribution of operational staff that know the business first hand. The ideal member of a change team will also have good interpersonal skills, with an ability to listen as well as to communicate. This team will share a common purpose and will communicate that purpose to the rest of the organisation (Pendlebury, Grouard and Meston, 1998). It has the responsibility to link people to the strategic objective so that the desired change may be implemented. In smaller organisations, or with smaller changes, it is sufficient to process the change through existing structures. However, if your team is a division of a bigger organisation, make sure you get a representative onto the change team!

Making changes on your team

So far the main emphasis has been on significant change; imposed change that is handed down from a higher or external force. However, it may be that you just want to do a little tinkering with your team. If so the same principles apply but you will have a little more scope in the methodology you employ. There is an opportunity to take a more facilitative approach by using a participative model of change management.

Say, for example, you want to re-organise your team from a generic to a key worker system where certain staff are given primary responsibility for a set of clients. Use the team meeting to make your case for how things can be improved. Employ your group work skills by leading, guiding, supporting, building trust, co-ordinating and communicating effectively. A team that is functioning well will be receptive to this for it will already have the basic ingredients of trust, openness, camaraderie and a sense of common purpose.

Involve everyone in the process. Take a workshop approach by facilitating participation. Use a flip chart to gather all ideas, no matter how far fetched. Put in a ground rule that no one can criticise another's contribution at this stage. Banish negative comment.

Next get the team to consider and evaluate the ideas based on their ultimate benefit to the client (Stewart, 1996). Naturally, there will be a tendency for staff to focus on the implications for themselves. This is a legitimate, but not a primary, consideration. The customer, however, must come first. Therefore, the first question should be; would service delivery be improved by this change? Once you have established the benefits of the proposed change move on to the other considerations. There may be implications in terms of time, money, training or other resources such as accommodation or equipment (Galpin, 1996).

Set team objectives and, where possible, allow individuals to set personal objectives. Some individuals may require a little coaching, that is to say some one-to-one support (Pendlebury, Grouard and Meston, 1998). Coaching, derived from sports, helps people to embrace change and take risks. It promotes one's ability to survive in complex and uncertain situations; in other words, it fosters resilience. People are tough. In the theory of evolution the best species survived by adapting to their environment. However, human kind went one better and changed the environment.

Since this is not an imposed change you may want to put a toe in the water first before going completely live. You could pilot the change with a few members of staff first. Pilots are a great way of winning staff support for change. There is no big bang and staff have time to acclimatise to the change. You are able to give the message that, if it does not work, you will drop the whole idea, so people are generally more relaxed about it. I have known pilot projects to go on for twenty years! Build in a system for measuring success by knowing the outcomes you want to achieve (Heller, 1998).

Annabel Broome (1998) has developed a very helpful **model for managing your own change project** and is summarised here as follows:

1. *Open system analysis*: identify your current management concerns. Are you happy with your role and your team's performance?
2. *Defining the future*: What demand do you want the change to have on your unit?
3. *What changes are needed?*
4. *Forcefield analysis*: What are the forces for and against the change?
5. *Environmental mapping*: Identify key people and rate their readiness and capability.
6. *Readiness and capability*: How ready are the key people to change in the way you want?
7. *Self assessment*: What skill, influence and motivation do you bring to the change process?
8. *Building a desire for change*: The individual and the team will be more ready to change if the level of change is neither too high nor too low.
9. *Transition*: What have you done to prepare for the shock and resistance?
10. *Transition plans*: What are your plans for managing the period of change, the integration of your team during the change and the future?
11. *Building commitment*: What is your plan for this and what key individuals have you identified?
12. *Responsibility for transition planning*: Take those directly involved and identify and assign tasks.
13. *Evaluation*: What are the transformations you wanted to make and how will you know they were made?
14. *Boundaries*: Who else do you need to communicate with, and who do you need to inform, persuade or instruct?

Common pitfalls

There are a number of common reasons why change initiatives can fail. As alluded to earlier, it will fail if there was not a sufficient reason for the change in the first place. If you cannot state the reason why in one succinct sentence, you probably cannot do it either. Taking things too quickly is another common mistake. Staff really do need time to absorb what is going on and to have an opportunity to have a say. Coercion will usually provoke people and promote resistance. Remember, Joe Hill (the well known trade unionist, song writer and campaigner for many working class causes in the USA, who while campaigning for the right to free speech was framed on a murder charge and executed in 1915) is as alive as you and me. Non-consultation is a good way to rile people and bog things down in a mire of industrial relations. The adoption of a partnership approach is a more civilised approach to modern management. A 'flavour of the month' approach to change often results in failure as it results in a poor track record where staff confidence is lost. If those in charge do not get a sufficient level of 'buy in' from staff through the development of commitment, the change process will go nowhere. Likewise an absence, or withdrawal, of sponsorship from senior management for a change you want to make will see your blooming idea wither on the vine (Broome, 1998).

Main messages

- Change is doing things differently than they were before.
- A fundamental reason for change is a belief that things can be done better.
- The old order will not go quietly – manage resistance gently.
- Fear of the unknown is a big factor in the resistance of change.
- The flip side of resistance is commitment – harness it.
- Uncertainty is worse than bad news – keep people informed.
- The change process needs to be led from the front – that's you.
- There needs to be a convincing case for making a change (if it ain't broke, don't fix it).
- If you can't describe the reason for change in a few short sentences you probably shouldn't be making it.
- Personalise things for people – explain what it will mean for them.

Chapter 7

Managing Yourself

Know Thyself

Inscription on the Oracle of Apollo in the Temple at Delphi

Knowing yourself

Greek mythology has it that people would come from far and wide to consult the oracle at Delphi where it was customary to seek predictions of one's destiny. If the tourists, who still flock to Delphi, wanted to consult an oracle nowadays they are probably more likely to go online. Philosophers such as Socrates and Plato subsequently took up the maxim. It came to signify learning to be one's self in all respects. This is akin to some modern psychological concepts such as wholeness and the complete self. Most successful managers have good self-awareness. They know their strengths and weaknesses and tend to build their careers by using and developing their natural talents. Think of professional athletes; they stood out from their peers in their chosen field when they were children. As they practiced their talents grew, and so did their confidence. They received specialist training to enhance their skills and develop their talent. However, even the best athlete is not necessarily much better than their competitors. In a sprint a gold medal might be separated from silver by the tiniest fraction of a second

We tend to choose our career paths by following our talents. Therefore a school leaver who is good at mathematics is more likely to become an accountant than a writer. One who is good at literature is more likely to become a writer than an accountant. It follows that best results can be had by the use of one's best skills. It is a good career move to identify as early as possible where your particular talent lies and then to develop it. Achievers seldom model themselves on others (Wadsworth, 1997). If you are weak in a particular area, and it matters for the job you are currently in, seek out the appropriate training and fill the deficit. Conversely, if you are strong in a particular area, specialise in it and make it your own area of expertise. This is equivalent to 'cornering a market' in the business world.

Social care training and practice emphasises the innate ability of an individual to change. In the same way, do not underestimate your own capacity to develop and enhance your capabilities. However, do not set yourself up for failure by biting off more than you can chew; and do not beat yourself up if you do not get it just right on every occasion (McBride and Clark, 1996). Perfection makes a better aspiration than it does an acquisition; so do not set your sights too high. Like an athlete, banish negative thoughts and experience the truly awesome power of positive thinking. By envisioning yourself as you want to be you are already on the road to self-achievement.

My mother, when she meets a man that impresses her (and it's always a man) will say; 'That's a fine fellow'. The phrase encapsulates a sense of decency, honour, respect, humour and self-assurance. In other words the guy has character. The essence of character is the moral choices that one makes. Consider what Dumbledore once said to Harry Potter: 'It is our choices, Harry, that show what we truly are, far more than our abilities' (Rowling, 1998).

Being principled is essential for sustained success in our chosen walk of life. Cutting corners may make short-term gains, but a bad reputation is hard to lose and can linger long after one has tried to make amends. Therefore it pays to act with integrity. Integrity is adherence to a moral code that values honesty and responsibility. Managers are faced with dilemmas and ethical conundrums all the time and the decisions taken should be based on a moral foundation. A good manager will instil a sense of integrity into the culture of the team. This promotes a climate of honesty and trust that will encourage open communication and a sense of loyalty. Loyalty is what glues a team together and distinguishes it from other, disconnected, groups.

As a manager you have to stand for something of worth, so operate on a platform of values. Draw up a set of values for yourself that you are not prepared to compromise or yield. The list may include some of the following (McBride and Clark, 1996; Wadsworth, 1997):

- Family comes first.
- Always let your conscience be your guide.

- Pursue job satisfaction through meaningful work.
- Be positive always.
- Your decisions have consequences for others.
- Commit to life long learning.
- Promote the success of subordinates.
- Do the best you can with what you have.
- Do not settle for less than you can achieve.
- Take responsible risks without fear of failure.

Making the most of yourself

The basic rule of thumb is that if you cannot manage yourself well you will not be able to manage others well (Bolt, 1999). Most of us will have had the experience at some point of a boss who was too busy to get organised. They fly about in a frenzy of busyness, never planning ahead and always picking up and running with whatever lands under their nose. They will call snap meetings to address the latest crisis and then cancel them because something even more apocalyptic has occurred. They will not have the clarity to tell you exactly what they want, but anything you prepare for them will always be too little too late. Such people do not have, or deserve, the respect of their staff; not that they will notice.

To avoid becoming such a manager it is important to be constantly aware of your own performance. Hard work alone is not enough; you can spend a lot of time running around in circles. You have got to manage for results. Again, you do not have to be a perfectionist but a diligent application of high standards is a must. This comes back to knowing your strengths and weaknesses. Use your talents to produce the best outcomes.

Be aware of your accountability to the organisation. At a certain level your organisation will be more concerned with what you do rather than how you do it. In other words, you will not be actively managed so it is all the more important that you manage yourself. Always take full responsibility for your actions and those of your team.

It pays to give some consideration to how others perceive you. Your concept of being helpful to a staff member might be their concept of you being a control freak. So, seek feedback and be aware that perceptions can change. Through ongoing self-development your performance can change too if needs be. Self-development is an intrinsic element of management development.

Management is not a single-handed occupation, so always be mindful of those around you. Include staff in what you do. You will achieve a lot more working with people than without them. Trust people, to whom you delegate responsibilities (Stewart, 1997). Yet, as President Ronald Reagan used to say, 'trust but verify'.

Remember to put a little urgency into the proceedings; this is a healthy energy as opposed to the panic-stricken approach of the bewildered manager. Always maintain a positive frame of mind and do not be put off by set backs. Avoid any temptation to get set in your ways. Successful managers are always on their toes, eager for changes and new challenges. Take reasonable risks: it is better to take a few knocks along the way than to spend your career in an armchair of inactivity.

In making the most of yourself, your understanding of your performance will be improved by answering the following questions:

- Can I articulate my own values in an unambiguous manner?
- Can I communicate my values to others?
- What are my strengths and weaknesses?
- How well do I cope with unexpected challenges?
- How well do I receive constructive criticism?
- Can I keep sight of the bigger picture?
- Can I bring others along with me?
- Do I have a positive attitude?

Finally, ask yourself the big question, what personal achievements would I like them to list in my obituary? (Wadsworth, 1997)

Organising yourself

Remember the old slogan, I wanted to go out and change the world but I couldn't find a baby-sitter? Most of us accept that we are not going to change the world, but it would be nice to be responsible for changing just a little bit of it. Everyone who goes into social care does so because they want to make a difference. However, achieving this requires organisation. The first thing you have got to do is set yourself clear goals and objectives.

Set out in explicit terms what it is you want to achieve and by when. Efficiency is not enough; you can do all the wrong things with great efficiency. You need to be effective as well and that requires you to be clear about what outcomes you are looking for. Be proactive when you are setting objectives for yourself, otherwise you will get stuck in the here and now. Set time frames that may be short term, medium term or long term. Therefore, you can set yourself tasks for each day, week, month or year.

It helps to reflect on your mission when planning what to do. Keeping a focus on your long term purpose can give great meaning to the things you have to do each day (Linacre, 1997). Also, by managing with vision you are taking into account the longer-term effects of the decisions you are currently making.

Set out to earn a reputation as someone who gets things done. Picture yourself reaching your goals; it is a powerful source of motivation (Bolt, 1999). Be conscious of the fact that brownie points have a short shelf-life: you are as good as your last performance, so keep re-setting goals and set out to achieve them.

As well as spending time on organising yourself in your current job, consider where it is that you want to ultimately wind up. After closer consideration you may decide that you do not want to go there. For example, you may have an eye on a promotion. This brings with it more responsibility. It may also bring more grief in the form of longer hours, more unpredictability, travel and hob-knobbing with types you do not like. Is this what you want?

Organising your day

The old maxim 'never put off until tomorrow what you can do today', is wise counsel. Plan tomorrow's work today (Linacre, 1997). Do this last thing before you go home. Not only will this make you more efficient and effective; it will also greatly reduce your anxiety because it brings closure to your working and clarity regarding the coming day.

To avoid everyday work piling up on you prioritise what it is you have to do. Set realistic deadlines. Do one thing at a time and give it your full attention. It requires a bit of self-training to block out everything else, particularly in a pressurised environment, but it is a skill worth having. Handle each piece of paper only once, marking it for action required, information, filing or dumping. Use a highlighter pen to mark the salient points.

Do not pile things up on your desk. I have a theory that the state of a person's desk has a direct co-relation to the state of their mind. So put everything in its rightful place, and make sure you have a filing system that is logical and where things can be easily retrieved. Do not file anything you do not need; do not be afraid to bin things. Binning is good. Arrange for an annual audit of the filing system and get rid of anything that is not needed.

Do not postpone unpalatable tasks. Tackle the most unpleasant task first thing in the morning; then the rest of the day can only get better (Kelly, 1988). Use your diary as a tool to help you organise yourself. When you are scheduling meetings put in an end time as well as a start time. Bunch your phone calls together, and do it early in the day. In that way, you will get more done sooner, and if someone has to phone you back it increases the likelihood of them doing so within the same day. Always return phone calls, or get someone else to do it where appropriate. There is nothing more irritating than someone declining to return a call. Resist the temptation to open all your e-mails as they come in. Instead, schedule time to deal with them. There is logic in doing this after you have made your phone calls, on the same basis that there is the rest of the day for people to get back to you, or for you to take necessary action in response to the e-mail.

Make a 'to do list'. Nowadays there are many software packages available, but it is hard to beat an A4 sheet of paper and a pencil. Draw a line down the middle of it listing e-mails and calls to make on the left and all other tasks on the right. Then prioritise them and give them a due date.

Diary 'thinking time'. As manager it falls to you to do the forward planning. It is all too easy to preoccupy yourself with the here and now at the expense of the future. Find a quiet space, preferably away from your office, to spend some quality time working up those big ideas. I had a boss once who lived a few hours drive from the office. Occasionally he would take the train to work. Those were the days when you knew he would arrive in the office completely up to speed about everything, and he also used the time to hatch a cunning plan or two. Consequently, on those days, the word would go around the office: 'He's taking the train!'

Managing time

Apart from your staff, time is your most valuable asset. It is the one thing that is always disappearing so you must use it well (Linacre, 1997). It is all too easy to spend a disproportionate amount of time on the things we like, or avoiding the things we do not like. The trick, therefore, is to make sure that you are spending time on the things that matter most, whether you like them or not. This requires a keen sense of purpose. Be clear about what it is you are supposed to be doing and do not waste time on peripheral issues. Focus on the things you can do something about because to do otherwise is a waste of time (McBride and Clark, 1996). Set yourself five or six priorities for each day and work your way through them. Gauge the size of the tasks so that you can get them finished within the day. However, if you have to leave a task unfinished place it on top of your priority list for the following day.

Make time to tackle the big jobs, even when they are not yet nipping at your heels. Given the immediacy and, often, the urgency of the delivery of social care it would be no trouble at all to give away this quality time to a bit more fire-fighting. However, train yourself to resist and you will manage better in the end. Pick an optimum time of day when you know you are more likely to have plenty of energy, so that you can take a real run and jump at the task (Adair, 2004). Take regular breaks, at least five minutes every forty-five when you are working on a big job. Take in fresh air during these breaks, if it is available to you; it will help to top up your batteries.

Scrap all useless activities. Be ruthless about this and really challenge yourself. When you clarify your priorities and key responsibilities the unproductive activities will become more obvious. Restrict yourself to doing what you alone can do. Delegate everything else, as described in Chapter 3. However, when you delegate a task always set a return date on which to receive the job back.

Cut out time wasters. Telephone interruptions can be a real waste of time. A telephone is of no assistance if you do not use it correctly. So, take control of it. Ideally you should have someone handling your incoming calls. In this way they can be filtered, banked and then responded to in a block of time. Ban telephones from your 'thinking time' as they would water down the quality of the session when you really want to be single minded. Mobile phones are a great invention but it amazes me how people allow themselves to be subjugated by them. For example, someone can go to the trouble of attending a meeting and then continue to receive calls on their mobile during it. If someone seeks a meeting with you and then takes a call in front of you show them the door because you and they, apparently, have something more important to be doing.

Another time waster is the persistent, uninvited, visitor. You should distinguish this from the occasional, neighbourly, visit which is a good means of socialising, exchanging information and keeping you off of the ivory tower. However, people who frequently interrupt are not helpful. They are not there to help you solve your problems; they are there to get you to solve their problems. It is said that a businessman in my neighbourhood has no chair on the other side of his desk. That is one way of helping people keep to the point. If you do get an uninvited guest and it really is not convenient, head them off at the pass by getting in first and politely telling them that you are up to your neck with a problem of your own, but make a commitment to get back to them at a time that is convenient to both of you.

Only go to meetings when you really have to as the travel time alone can consume huge amounts of time. Be a stickler for punctuality and agree a time by which the meeting should end. Remember, you can have meetings on the telephone. Use new technologies if you can, such as teleconferencing, videoconferencing and net meetings.

Finally, your schedule needs to be flexible enough to expect the unexpected. This might take the form of summons from your boss, or it may be a crisis that requires your immediate attention. Either way, if you organise your time well, the unexpected will become easier to manage and you will find it easier to re-schedule your time.

Assertiveness

Assertiveness is getting your point across honestly and clearly while at the same time respecting the feelings of other people. Successful managers are clear about what they want and are focused about going out and getting it (Wadsworth, 1997). They are direct, without being abrasive. They will not avoid confrontation, but neither will they seek it. They will be well able to articulate their views and assert their rights without feeling the need to trail their coat. Assertiveness is that perfect place between aggression and passiveness.

It is important to recognise your own needs and to know where you are on the spectrum of assertiveness. You will already have a fair idea. Are you, for example, comfortable about returning faulty goods to a store, and would you prefer to put up with a bad meal rather than complain about it? If the answer is yes then you need to work on your assertiveness skills. Passiveness will not get you what you want. It leads to tolerating violations of your own rights while you reason with yourself that the issue was not important enough to make a fuss about. Passive behaviour can also mean that you express a view, but you do it so meekly that it can easily be overturned or disregarded (Stubbs, 1997). It also means that saying no will not come easily. If you are on this end of the spectrum, practice your assertiveness. The trick is to express what you want clearly and openly using non-judgemental language to make your point. Stick to the facts, and do not feel that you have to argue your case. So, go into training and set yourself some challenges.

Aggressive behaviour invades other people's space and violates their rights (Stubbs, 1997). Aggressive people have little regard for the feelings of others. Aggressive managers are more concerned with the bottom line than they are with people. Not only are they prepared to state their case forcibly but also they are prepared to use coercive tactics to get what they want. A hallmark of the aggressive manager is that they show no respect for more junior staff. No one is likely to describe oneself as aggressive. However, if you find that you actually enjoy bringing faulty goods back to the store and complaining about lousy meals; if, in fact, you enjoy a good scrap, you may need to tone it down a little. As with passive personalities, the acid test is to state your case honestly and factually while at the same time being respectful to others. Put yourself in the other person's shoes. It is not all about winning; it is about finding solutions that accommodate everyone.

Good communication is the key to getting on with people. As well as stating your case calmly and clearly, listen to what other people are saying, and to what they are not saying. Most social care workers are trained to be active listeners, so draw on those skills. Use supportive responses such as reassurance, praise and persuasion. Avoid threatening responses such as ordering, warning or judging. Find the common ground between you and the other person. At the end of the day, interacting with others is not just giving or taking, it is about give *and* take.

Stress

We all need a level of stress to get us out of bed in the morning. Stress is beneficial when it motivates us to do better, like a football player who is pumped up before a game. Stress only becomes destructive when one experiences a loss of control as this induces a state of distress. Factors contributing to stress include work overload, conflicting priorities, unsupportive work environment, crisis management as a result of poor planning and career uncertainty. Stress may be triggered by personality factors, such as unrealistic expectations of one's self. Organisational culture can also play a part. For example, hierarchal bureaucracies or highly competitive work environments, both of which tend to have an 'everyone for themselves' mentality, can be contributors to stress. The onset of stress is brought about by an imbalance between demands made of one's personal resources (personality, attitude, skills) and external resources (support, coaching) to deal with those demands (McBride and Clark, 1996). It is a response to an inordinate amount of pressure.

Stress is cumulative in nature, and in the long term it can lead to circumstances such as severe loss of interest and commitment, or avoidance behaviours such as frequent absences. It may also present as an opposite extreme such as the 'workaholic' who sees working harder as the only solution. Workaholics cannot prioritise; they work obsessively, often on the wrong things. Ultimately such behaviour leads to burnout. Burnout has been described as a state of emotional exhaustion, a feeling of low personal accomplishment with clients and a sense of depersonalisation typified by an uncaring attitude towards clients (Maslach and Leiter, 2000).

The best way to deal with stress is to control the things you have the ability to control. Setting goals and priorities will help, as will concentrating on one task at a time. Work on skills that will assist you to keep things under control, such as asserting yourself to say no when you mean no. Delegate upwards when the need arises and do not feel you have to carry the can for everything. Do not seek perfection; that last ten per cent is just not worth the effort (Wadsworth, 1997). A good job does not have to be perfect.

Stop worrying; it is a futile occupation. Either do something about the issue that is troubling you or forget about it. If it comes to it, it is better to stay back in the office for a few hours to resolve a problem than to go home and fret about it all night. However, make this an exception rather than a rule. Put right what you can by identifying the stress factors and consider what your options are in terms of dealing with them.

It is best to accept the things you cannot control. In any event, these will be far less plentiful when you control what you can (Adair, 2004). It is important to be able to detach from the stresses of work. I once worked in offices where a psychiatrist, in moments of high pressure, would lock himself away in the bathroom and play a few soothing tunes on his tin whistle! So, find your own mechanism to unwind and indulge yourself occasionally.

When the time comes to go home, do just that and leave the troubles of the day behind. It is important to develop the ability to let go, but this may require a little application. Take a little time between office and home to debrief yourself. Have you ever had the experience of driving home from work and then not being able to remember any part of the journey? That is because you were still psychologically back at the office. Find your way of unwinding. Relaxation techniques, often taught on social care programmes, are a proven way of reducing stress and promoting a sense of well-being. Create your own sanctuary; a little bubble of peaceful space just for you (Roland, 2000). You could always resort to what a former tutor of mine used to refer to as 'a good dollop of whiskey', but that is definitely not to be recommended as a positive solution.

Work/life balance

Money, according to an old Latin teacher of mine, is the root of all evil, but at least it allows you to be miserable in comfort! Most of us, every so often, dream of winning the lottery. But it does beg the question, what would we do all day if we did not have to get up in the morning and have to go to work to earn a living? We need to be clear about what we consider to be the real purpose of our lives. What we do for a living is, no doubt, an important factor in our overall makeup. As well as providing a living it also confers social status, but it does not fully define us as individuals. Therefore, balancing our work with other areas of our lives is an important issue.

Other areas of life need not be defined strictly in terms of responsibilities such as child or elder care, but may include social or personal activities. It is important, therefore, to have objectives and aspirations in those other areas of our lives. These areas might include social life, sport and leisure, hobbies, self-improvement, community activity or spiritual or religious interests (Wadsworth, 1997). Down time from work provides recovery and opportunities to invest in other valuable areas of our lives.

Children do not dream of becoming a manager (Watson and Harris, 1999). They are much more likely to opt for fire-fighting or football. Perhaps the really lucky ones are those who can construct a life around what they consider to be really important and then to be able to make a living from it, such as a successful sports personality. In such circumstances money is a by-product, not an end in itself. Within human service organisations too money is often not a primary motivation. One chooses a career in the caring professions and issues such as money and promotion are secondary, coming behind job satisfaction, recognition and a personal sense of achievement. Advancement into management from a profession is never an original career intention.

Working longer hours seems to go with the territory of being a manager nowadays. This is not necessarily a bad thing if it is kept under reasonable control. New managers can adjust to working longer hours once it is in the context of an appropriate work/life balance. It becomes hazardous, however, if there is an organisational culture that routinely expects this of their managers. Indeed, there is plenty of evidence to suggest that promotions are handed out as rewards to those who are prepared to work all the hours. In effect this is a form of manipulation, as it constitutes a cost benefit to the employer at the expense of the employee. It is far more productive to focus on quality and outcomes than it is to concentrate on being busy.

However, there is a growing recognition among organisations that staff need to be enabled if they are to recruit and retain motivated, productive and a less stressed workforce. Good people management recognises that organisational objectives can be served by facilitating the needs of employees. Employers of choice can be identified by their explicit recognition of staff and where their organisational values are clearly set out and demonstrated in deed.

Busy people who are going places often do not take time out to reflect on where they are at, or to thank their lucky stars for what they have got so far. The prize always seems to be in the future. However, it can be very empowering to take a little time out to reflect upon how good things are right now; to appreciate the really important things such as relationships, values and beliefs.

Managing your career

No doubt you entered social care for loftier reasons, but the stark fact remains that you are a marketable commodity. Your career path is nobody's responsibility but your own, so what you do with your skills and talents is up to you. Ask yourself; what do you want? It may be a quiet life, fame and money, recognition or a sense of self-fulfilment. Next question, what are you prepared to do to get it?

To get on in your career you need to identify your learning needs. Identify what skills you need and what levels of performance you need to set for yourself. Seek out learning opportunities on the job. This might come in the form of work delegated downward from your boss. Putting yourself forward for membership of working groups or special projects will also help to broaden your horizon. Get about more to other organisations, particularly ones that excel in areas related to your own service (Mayo, 1991). Develop a keen awareness of consumer perception in relation to need and client satisfaction. Employing the skills of an external mentor is a good way of getting independent feedback and advice.

Climbing metaphors tend to be used to describe career paths in terms of a vertical or hierarchical mobility (Watson and Harris, 1999). However career progression does not have to be viewed strictly as a ladder, with each higher rung having a better value than the one below. Fortunately, there are now more opportunities for social care workers to advance without necessarily progressing into management. Senior practitioner posts are one way of providing non-management career advancement to experienced workers. Furthermore, particularly in clinical posts, there are opportunities to combine clinical work with management work, where clinical managers retain a reduced caseload. Think of your career more as a terrain: there are high places and low points, there are boring parts and exciting areas, there are threats and opportunities. The question is; where do you want to be at this point in time?

Only you can define what success means for you. Fame and fortune are not ends in themselves. Genuine success and real achievement come from knowing what you want out of life and then setting goals to achieve them (Wadsworth, 1997). Management is making things happen.

Main messages

- Know yourself.
- If you can't manage yourself well you won't manage others well.
- Take reasonable risks – it's better to take a few knocks along the way than to spend your career in an armchair of inactivity.
- What personal achievements would you like to be mentioned in your obituary?
- Efficiency is not enough – you have to be effective as well.
- Never put off until tomorrow what you can do today.
- Do the most unpalatable task first thing in the morning; the rest of the day can only get better.
- Apart from staff, time is your most valuable asset – don't waste it.
- Get the work/life balance thing right.
- Genuine success comes from knowing what you want out of life and then setting goals to achieve it.

References

Adair, J. (1987) *Effective Teambuilding: How to Make a Winning Team.* London: Pan.

Adair, J. (2003) *Effective Strategic Leadership.* London: Pan Macmillan.

Adair, J. (2004) *The John Adair Handbook of Management and Leadership.* London: Thorogood.

Allen, J. (1996) *How to be Better at Motivating People.* London: Kogan Page.

Amos, J. (2000) *Making Meetings Work.* Oxford: Essentials.

Armstrong, M. (1999) *How to be an Even Better Manager.* 5th edn. London: Kogan Page.

Armstrong, M. and Baron, A. (2004) *Managing Performance: Performance Management in Action.* London: Chartered Institute of Personnel and Development.

Austin, D.M. (2002) *Human Service Management: Organisational Leadership in Social Work Practice.* New York: Columbia University Press.

Bandel, T., Boulter, L. and Kelly, J. (1994) *Implementing Quality in the Public Sector.* London: Pitman.

Barnado's (2006) *Mission Statement.* Wellington, NZ: Barnardo's.

Bee, F. and Bee, R. (2001) *Customer Care.* London: Chartered Institute of Personnel and Development.

Bilson, A. and Ross, S. (Eds.) (1999) *Social Work Management and Practice. Systems Principles.* London: Jessica Kingsley.

Bolt, P. (1999) *The Whole Manager: How to Succeed Without Selling Your Soul.* Dublin: Oak Tree Press.

Bone, D. and Griggs, R. (1989) *Quality at work.* London: Kogan Page.

Bowlby. J. (1969) *Attachment and Loss (Vol 1).* London: Basic Books.

Boyle, T. (1997) *Team Based Working.* Dublin: Institute of Public Administration.

Brocka, B. and Brocka, M.S. (1992) *Quality Management: Implementing the Best Ideas of the Masters.* Chicago: Irwin Professional Publishing.

Broome, A. (1998) *Managing Change.* 2nd edn. London: Macmillan.

Brown. H.C. (1996) in Vass, A.A. (Ed.) *Social Work Competencies: Core Knowledge, Values and Skills.* London: Sage.

Bruce, S.J. (1999) *Becoming an Effective Policy Advocate: From Policy to Practice to Social Justice.* Belmont, CA: Brooks/Cole.

Bryson, J.M. (Ed.) (1993) *Strategic Planning for Public and Not-for-Profit Organisations.* Oxford: Pergamon.

Bryson, J.M. and Farnum, K.A. (2005) *Creating and Implementing Your Strategic Plan: A Workbook for Public and Non-Profit Organisations.* San Francisco: John Wiley and Sons.

Bunker, D.R. and Wijnberg, M.A. (1988) *Supervision and Performance: Managing Professional Work in Human Service Organisations.* San Fransisco: Jossey Bass.

Butler, M. (2000) *Performance Measurement in the Health Sector.* Dublin: Institution of Public Administration.

Cartwright, R. (2000) *Mastering Customer Relations.* London: Macmillan.

Christian, W.P. and Hannah, G.T. (1983) *Effective Management in Human Services.* New Jersey: Prentice Hall.

Clarke, J. (1996) *A Guide to Self Evaluation.* Dublin: Combat Poverty.

Clarke, J. (1996) *Staff Support and Supervision.* Dublin: Combat Poverty.

Clarke, J. (1997) *Strategic Planning.* Dublin: Combat Poverty.

Cole, G.A. (2003) *Strategic Management: Theory and Practice.* London: Thomson Learning.

Courtney, R. (2002) *Strategic Management for Voluntary Non-Profit Organisations.* London: Routledge.

Cushway, B. (1994) *Human Resource Management.* London: Kogan Page. Fast Track MBA Series.

Davidson, J. (2001) *The Complete Idiot's Guide to Change Management.* New York: Penguin.

Department of Health (1998) *Modernising Social Services.* London: HMSO.

Department of Health (2000) *A Quality Strategy for Social Care.* London: HMSO.

Drucker, P.F. (1990) *Managing the Non-Profit Organisation: Priorities and Principles.* London: Butterworth Heineman.

Eales-White, R. (1996) *How to be a Better Team Builder.* London: Kogan Page.

Evard, B.L. and Gipple, C.A. (2001) *Managing Business Change for Dummies.* New York: Hungry Minds.

Eyre, E.C. (1992) *Mastering Basic Management.* London: Macmillan.

Firth, S., Luff, G. and Oliviere, D. (2005) *Facing Death: Loss, Change and Bereavement in Palliative Care.* Maidenhead: Open University Press.

Ford Foundation (2006) *Mission Statement.* New York: Ford Foundation.

Galpin, T.J. (1996) *The Human Side of Change: Practical Guide to Organisational Redesign.* San Francisco: Jossey Boss.

Gilbert, P. (2005) *Leadership: Being Effective and Remaining Human.* Lyme Regis: Russell House Publishing.

Great Britain (2003) *Change for the Better: Business Change for Decision Makers.* Norwich: Format Publishing.

Greenwood, E. (1957) Attributes of a Profession. *Social Work.* 2: 44–55.

Groom, W. (1994) *Gumpisims: The Wit and Wisdom of Forest Gump.* New York: Pocket Books.

Gunnigle, P. and Flood, P. (1990) *Personnel Management in Ireland.* Dublin: Gill and Macmillan.

Gunnigle, P., Heraty, N. and Morley, M. (1997) *Personnel and Human Resource Management: Theory and Practice in Ireland.* Dublin: Gill and Macmillan.

Handy, C. (1999) *Understanding Organisations.* 4th edn. London: Penguin.

Hannaway, C. and Hunt, G (1995) *The Management Skills Book.* Aldershot: Gower.

Hardy, G (1996) *Successfully Managing Change in a Week.* London: Headway.

Harlow, E. and Lawler, J. (Eds.) (2002) *Managing Social Work and Change.* Aldershot: Ashgate.

Harris, J. (2003) *The Social Work Business.* London: Routledge.

Harris, J. and Kelly. D. (1991) *Management Skills in Social Care: A Handbook for Social Care Managers.* Aldershot: Gower.

Harvard Business Review (1998) *Harvard Business Review on Change.* Boston, MA.

Heller, R. (1998) *Managing Change.* Dorling Kindersley.

Honey, P. (1992) *Problem People and How to Manage Them.* London: Chartered Institute of Personnel Management.

Hussey, D.E. (2000) *How to Manage Organisational Change.* London: Kogan Page.

Kadushin, A. (1992) *Supervision in Social Work.* New York: Columbia University Press.

Kelly, A. (1988) *How to Make Your Life Easier at Work.* 2nd edn. New York: McGraw Hill.

Kenefick, D. (1998) in McAuliffe, E. and Joyce, L. (Eds.) *A Healthier Future? Managing Healthcare in Ireland.* Dublin: Institute of Public Administration.

Kenny, I. (2003) *Can You Manage?* Dublin: Oak Tree Press.

Kettner, P.M., Moroney, R.M. and Martin L.L. (1999) *Designing and Managing Programs an Effectiveness-Based Approach.* Thousand Oaks, CA: Sage.

Koteen, J. (1997) *Strategic Management in Public and Non-Profit Organisations.* Westport, CN. Praeger.

Lord Laming (2003) *Victoria Climbié Inquiry Report.* London: HMSO.

Lawrence, L.M. and McKettner, P. (1996) *Measuring the Performance of Human Service Programs.* London: Sage.

Lawrence, P. (1986) *Invitation to Management.* New York: Basil Blackwell.

Leland, K. and Bailey, K. (1999) *Customer Service for Dummies.* New York: Hungry Minds.

Lewis, J. et al. (2001) *Management of Human Service Programs.* 3rd edn. Belmont, CA: Brooks/Cole Thomson Learning.

Linacre, N. (1997) *The Successful Executive.* London: Century.

Luffman, G., Lea, E. and Sanderson, S. (1998) *Strategic Management: An Analytical Introduction.* Oxford: Blackwell.

MacDonald, J. (2003) *Understanding Total Quality Management in a Week.* 3rd edn. London: Hodder and Stoughton.

Martin, L.L. and Kettner, P.M. (1996) *Measuring the Performance of Human Service Programs.* London: Sage.

Martin, V. and Henderson, E. (2001) *Managing in Health and Social Care.* London: Routledge.

Maslach, C. and Leiter, M. (2000) *Preventing Burnout and Building Engagement: A Complete Program for Organisational Renewal.* San Fransisco: Jossey Bass.

Mayo, A. (1991) *Managing Careers: Strategies for Organisations.* London: Chartered Institute of Personnel Management.

McBride, J. and Clark, N. (1996) *20 Steps to Better Management.* London: BBC.

Mintzberg, H. and Quinn, B. (1992) *The Strategy Process: Concepts and Contexts.* Hemel Hampstead: Prentice-Hall.

Morrison, T. (1999) *Staff Supervision in Social Care.* Brighton: Pavilion.

Murdock, A. (2003) *Personal Effectiveness.* 3rd edn. London: Butterworth Heinemann.

National Association of Social Workers (1999) *Code of Ethics.* Washington, DC: NASW.

Northern Area Health Board (2004) *Professional Supervision Policy and Procedures.* Dublin.

O'Connor, M., Mangan, J. and Cullen, J. (Eds.) (1994) *IMI Handbook of Management.* Dublin: Oak Tree Press.

O'Sullivan, T. (1999) *Decision Making in Social Work.* London: Macmillan.

Oakland, J. and Morris, P. (1998) *Pocket Guide to Total Quality Management.* London: Butterworth Heinmann.

Osborne, S.P. (Ed.) (1996) *Managing in the Voluntary Sector: A Handbook for Managers in Charitable and Non-Profit Organisations.* London: International Thomson Business Press.

Pendlebury, J., Grouard, B. and Meston, F. (1998) *The 10 Keys to Successful Change Management.* Chichester: John Wiley & Sons.

Roebuck, C. (1998) *Effective Communication: The Essential Guide to Thinking and Working Smarter.* London: Marshall Publications.

Roland, P. (2000) *How to Meditate.* London: Hamlyn.

Rooney, R.H. (1992) *Strategies for Work With Involuntary Clients.* New York: Columbia University Press.

Rowling, J.K. (1998) *Harry Potter and the Chamber of Secrets.* London: Bloomsbury.

Salvation Army (2006) *Salvation Army Mission Statement.* London: The Salvation Army.

Sarri, R.C. and Hasenfeld,Y. (1978) (Eds.) *The Management of Human Services.* New York: Columbia Press.

Sayles, L.R. (1979) *Leadership: What Effective Managers Really do and How They do it.* New York: McGraw Hill.

Scott, C.D. and Jaffe, D.T. (1990) *Managing Organisational Change: A Guide for Managers.* London: Kogan Page.

Scragg, T. (2001) *Managing at the Front Line: A Handbook for Managers in Social Care Agencies.* Brighton: Pavilion.

Smith, R.J (1994) *Strategic Management and Planning in the Public Sector.* London: Longman.

Social Information Systems Ltd (2005) *Workload Management.* Cheshire: Unpublished.

Soriano, F.L. (1995) *Conducting Needs Assessments: A Multi-Disciplinary Approach.* California: Sage.

Statham, D. (2004) (Ed.) *Managing Front Line Practice in Social Care.* London: Jessica Kingsley.

Stewart, J. (1996) *Managing Change Through Training and Development.* 2nd edn. London: Kogan Page.

Stewart, R. (1997) *The Reality of Managing.* London: Butterworth Heinemann.

Stubbs, D.R. (1997) *Assertiveness at Work.* London: Pan.

Vass, A. (Ed.) (1996) *Social Work Competancies: Core Knowledge, Values and Skills.* London: Sage.

Wadsworth, W.J (1997) *The Agile Managers Guide to Goal-Setting and Achievement.* Briston: Velocity Business Publishing.

Walters, M. (Ed.) (1995) *The Performance Management Handbook.* London: Chartered Institute of Personnel and Development.

Watson, T. and Harris, P. (1999) *The Emergent Manager.* London: Sage.

Weinbach, R.W. (1994) *The Social Worker as Manager: Theory and Practice.* 2nd edn. Needam Heights: Allyn & Bacon.

Williams, N. (2003) *Unconditional Success: Living the Work we Were Born to do.* London: Brenton Books.

Recommended Reading and Websites

Management in general

Bolt, P. (1999) *The Whole Manager: How to Succeed Without Selling Your Soul.* Dublin: Oak Tree Press.

Handy, C. (1999) *Understanding Organisations.* 4th edn. London: Penguin.

Hannaway, C. and Hunt, G. (1995) *The Management Skills Book.* Aldershot: Gower.

McBride, J. and Clark, N. (1996) *20 Steps to Better Management.* London: BBC.

Wadsworth, W.J. (1997) *The Agile Manager's Guide to Goal-Setting and Achievement.* Briston: Velocity Business Publishing.

Management of social care

Austin, D.M. (2002) *Human Service Management: Organisational Leadership in Social Work Practice.* New York: Columbia University Press.

Bryson, J.M. and Farnum, K.A. (2005) *Creating and Implementing Your Strategic Plan: A Workbook for Public and Non-Profit Organisations.* San Francisco: John Wiley and Sons.

Bunker, D.R. and Wijnberg, M.A. (1998) *Supervision and Performance: Managing Professional Work in Human Service Organisations.* San Fransisco, CA: Jossey Bass.

Drucker, P.F. (1990) *Managing the Non-Profit Organisation: Priorities and Principles.* London: Heineman.

Harris, J. and Kelly, D. (1991) *Management Skills in Social Care: A Handbook for Social Care Managers.* Aldershot: Gower.

Koteen, J. (1997) *Strategic Management in Public and Non-Profit Organisations.* Westport, CT: Praeger.

Martin, V. and Henderson, E. (2001) *Managing in Health and Social Care.* London: Routledge.

Sarri, R.C. and Hasenfeld, Y. (1978) (Eds.) *The Management of Human Services.* New York: Columbia Press.

Scragg, T. (2001) *Managing at the Front Line: A Handbook for Managers in Social Care Agencies.* Brighton: Pavilion.

Statham, D. (2004) (Ed.) *Managing Front Line Practice in Social Care.* London: Jessica Kingsley.

Vass, A. (Ed.) (1996) *Social Work Competancies: Core Knowledge, Values and Skills.* Thousand Oaks, CA: Sage.

Weinbach. R.W. (1994) *The Social Worker as Manager: Theory and Practice.* London: Longman.

Specific aspects of management

Adair, J. (1987) *Effective Teambuilding: How to Make a Winning Team.* London: Pan.

Adair, J. (2003) *Effective Strategic Leadership.* London: Pan Macmillan.

Broome, A. (1998) *Managing Change.* 2nd edn. London: Macmillan.

Butler, M. (2000) *Performance Measurement in the Health Sector.* Dublin: Institution of Public Administration.

Davidson, J. (2001) *The Complete Idiot's Guide to Change Management.* New York: Penguin.

Gilbert, P. (2005) *Leadership: Being Effective and Remaining Human.* Lyme Regis: Russell House Publishing.

Oakland, J. and Morris, P. (1998) *Pocket Guide to Total Quality Management.* London: Butterworth.

Useful websites

British Association of Social Workers. (practice issues and publications) www.basw.co.uk

Department of Health (Social Care) (policies and publications) www.doh.gov.uk/scg/socialc.htm

Department of Health and Human Services (USA) (useful statistics, information and links) www.hhs.gov/

Irish Association of Social Workers (principles/code of ethics and publications) www.iasw.ie

International Federation of Social Workers (global organisation for best practice and international co-operation) www.ifsw..org/home

National Association of Social Workers (USA) (largest professional association for social work in the world) www.naswdc.org

National Institute for Social Work (policy, research and news) www.nisw.org.uk

Social Care Institute for Excellence (SCIE) (quality in practice and management) www.scie.org.uk